So That the Poem Remains

To Katie...
with bestwishes...
& looking forward
to your published book!
Salaam سلام

So That the Poem Remains

مع أطيب ...

Ghada Alatrash

March 2013

حَتّى تَبقى القَصيدة

Arabic Poems by Lebanese-American

Youssef Abdul Samad

Selected and Translated by

Ghada Alatrash

العالرابطة القلمية الجديدة

New Pen League

Agio
PUBLISHING HOUSE

Agio
PUBLISHING HOUSE

151 Howe Street, Victoria BC Canada V8V 4K5
in cooperation with

 الرابطة القلمية الجديدة

New Pen League

*For rights information and bulk orders, please contact
the publishers through* www.agiopublishing.com

So That the Poem Remains
ISBN 978-1-897435-81-6 (trade paperback)
ISBN 978-1-897435-82-3 (ebook)

Cataloguing information available from Library and Archives Canada.
Printed on acid-free paper.
Agio Publishing House is a socially responsible company,
measuring success on a triple-bottom-line basis.
10 9 8 7 6 5 4 3 2 1

To
Selma, Aamer and Marcel

...يا شمس المحبة حكايتنا أغزلي

O Sun of Love, weave our story... [1]

---

[1] A line taken from the song, *I am My Beloved's and My Beloved is Mine*, written and composed by Lebanese brothers Assi and Mansour Rahbani, and sung by Fairuz.

هذهِ الدنيا كتابٌ أنتَ فيهِ الفِكَرُ

هذهِ الدنيا ليالٍ أنتَ فيها العُمُرُ

هذهِ الدنيا عيونٌ أنتَ فيها البَصَرُ

هذهِ الدنيا سماءٌ أنتَ فيها القَمَرُ

"This life is a book and you are the thought.

This life is nights and you are the essence.

This life is eyes and you are the sight.

This life is a sky and you are the moon."[1]

---

[1]   A translated excerpt from a song written by Sudanese Poet Hadi Adam and sung by the legendary Egyptian singer, Umm Kulthum. The title of the song is: *Will I Meet You Tomorrow?*

TABLE OF CONTENTS

Introduction   i

 THE SPIRITUAL

And the Poem Remains	3
God Is Knowledge	11
Al Shqaif Hermitage	23
Give Us Back the Hoopoe	29
The July of Ages	35

THE POLITICAL

The Security Council	45
New York After the Storm	63
After the Murder of My Brother	69
Muntazar's Year	77
Perhaps If You Returned	91

ON WOMEN

To My Mother Who Left Me	99
Love, Poetry and Madness	109
When Noura is Saddened, the Rain Pours	119
O Muse of Poetry, Snatch Me Away	129
And the Question Remains	135
The Art Teacher	143
When You Awaken	153
The Night Became Still	161
More Than "I Love You"	167
Hermitage of the Soul	173

Introduction by Ghada Alatrash, *translator*

The East and the West: The Old and the New

"... I think it's great you're translating *his* poems because now I am able to read my father's work!"—These were the words of Linda Abdul Samad, the daughter of poet Youssef Abdul Samad, sent to me in an e-mail on an early morning in November 2011, a day when my awaited dreams were manifested in Linda's message.

Like Linda, many second generation immigrants, albeit able to speak and understand their parents' native tongue, are incapable of reading or writing it. I am a mother of three children (Selma, Aamer and Marcel) whose identities are amalgams of the East and the West, a blend of the old culture left behind in my native homeland of Syria and of the new Western culture in which we presently live.

The fact is that immigrants' children comprise a third culture, one that could perhaps be thought of as a hybrid product engendered by the fusion of different cultures. This third culture is one that preserves the pre-given cultural components acquired from the past and intermixes those components with the present ones, yielding a collective identity in a multicultural humanity.

After living as an Arab in the West for more than 25 years, I have come to believe passionately in this hybrid product as one that is beautiful, evolved and refined, taking the best ingredients from both worlds. It is a rich product that keeps a fine balance between the old and the new, a balance that could only be achieved by an active effort on our part as parents to teach our children the old but while at the same time embracing the new—to celebrate one's heritage and history while also partaking in the building of bridges that will connect each of our cultures with the universal human culture in which we live.

It is by translating this book that I am also endeavouring to participate in the building of bridges across cultures, hoping to connect between Linda's new culture and her father's old, between my children's and my own, between an English-speaking reader and an Arab poet, and ultimately, between the West and the East.

An Absence of the East

On another note, I believe that we, Arabs, have not been working diligently to deliver the true essence of our human civilization to the Western audience. Our languor has only done us a disservice and has played a part in the disfiguring of our image in the West. As Palestinian-American literary theorist Edward Said once explained, the blame falls on us Arabs for "the almost total absence" of any cultural position in the West to help either to identify with or dispassionately discuss our side.

In an English class during my high school days in Texas, I vividly recall the time when we came across a poem by Khalil Gibran in our textbook. At the sight of an Arab name, I was overcome by a sense of pride and nationalism as this poet happened to be the closest to my Syrian heritage and one obviously worthy of being taught in Western schools. But alas, this was an occurrence that seldom took place again in my subsequent academic years.

As I went on to pursue my graduate studies in literature, I found that my anthology texts were packed with names from all parts of the world except ours! *The Norton Anthology of Masterpieces* included names like Voltaire (French), Rousseau (Swiss), Tennyson (English), Dickinson (American), Tolstoy (Russian), Ibsen (Norwegian), Yeats (Irish), Pirandello (Italian), Kafka (German), Eliot (English-American), Garcia

Lorca (Spanish), Borges (Argentine), Narayan (Indian), Mishima (Japanese), Garcia Marquez (Colombian), Soyinka (Nigerian), etc. But there was never any mention of our endless literary list of Arab figures like Taha Hussain, Gassan Kanafani, Nagib Mahfouz, Ghada Samman, Hanna Meena, Ahlam Mustaghanmi, Nawal Al Saadawi, Tayyeb Saleh, Mahmoud Darwish, Abdul Rahman Munif, Mohammad Al Maghout, Elias Khoury and so on and so forth.

One of the reasons attributed to this imbalance, as explained by Said, is due to the fact that "Very little of the detail, the human density, the passion of Arab-Muslim life has entered the awareness of even those people whose profession it is to report the Arab world. What we have instead is a series of crude, essentialized caricatures of the Islamic world presented in such a way as to make that world vulnerable to military aggression."

Hence, my translation represents one of the many steps that must be taken in order to fill in for our cultural "absence" in the West. Perhaps the day will come when, as in the words of African revolutionist Amilcar Cabral, a "universal culture" will emerge based on "the critical assimilation of man's achievement in the domains of art, science, literature, etc," with the objective of "constant and generalized promotion of humanism, of solidarity, of respect and disinterested devotion to human beings."

On this Work of Translation

In this work of translation, I have chosen to present my readers with a wide selection of topics addressed by our poet Youssef Abdul Samad—the spiritual, the political, and what he wrote on women. Translating these poems was a delightful process, one that allowed me to journey the depth of the spiritual realms, to travel across political boundaries, and to dive into the amorous, flaming, and enchanted world of love and romance.

Poetry, as a form of expression of human feelings, becomes a common language for all regardless of nationality or background. However, as Robert Frost once wrote, "Poetry is what gets lost in translation"—a statement that holds very true and turns the process of translating into a matter of fidelity, of faithfulness to what was originally written. Hence, one of the most important objectives in the art of translation becomes to try to achieve the same effect that the poem had in its original language and awaken the feelings of the reader just as the original poet once did in his native tongue.

I once read that the process of translation is like moving a delicate piece of art from one place to another, where one hopes for the least damage possible. Indeed, poetry does not travel well, especially when moved across continents; it can easily become dishevelled and requires the most delicate care—a most challenging yet rewarding task.

Each of the poems I have chosen in this book is preceded with a few lines that represent my own reflection on the selected piece. In my translations, I endeavored not only to translate the literal context of the poem but also the emotional mood of the poet; moreover, I took the freedom (with the poet's permission) to make slight modifications in my English translation where I believed that a literal English translation did not capture the original meaning of the Arabic text. I hope to have captured the richness and depth that characterize the poet's style of writing.

I sincerely thank the poet for entrusting me with what was written by his heart of raw and genuine feelings. Abdul Samad possesses a most delicate and refined spirit, so sensitive that it could be scratched by the gentlest of winds. I also thank him for allowing me to taste the sweet pleasure that comes with translating poetry, to enter a haven only visited by poets and those who enjoy poetry, and to live up to my cause of bringing together the East and the West.

On the Poet

As for our poet, Youssef Abdul Samad was born in the pinelands of Lebanon, in a beautiful green village named Ras Al Maten. In 1969 he left his country for New York City, seeking education and experience.

Ever since, he has been travelling back and forth between the two worlds and the story of his life happens to be engraved on the trunks of the oldest Lebanese pine trees and written on the walls of the tallest buildings in New York. His heart is split into two halves, one dwelling in the East and the other in the West. "I am made of a blend of the two worlds; when I am in one place, I always find myself longing for the other," he says.

But Abdul Samad's travels were not only confined to the geographical boundaries drawn on the world map. The poet describes, with an unperturbed sense of calmness, how he has flown on the wings of poetry to spiritual worlds, to "secret hidden places of the soul" and to "the very bottom of things."

"Poetry awakens the deepest feelings in a human soul. Poetry is the language of the nightingales. It is the silence that is heard in the most profound discourse of nature. Poetry is the first rose we present to a beloved and the last we plant on the grave of the departed," he expresses.

Yet Abdul Samad makes clear that poetry has also pulled his spirit down to the most wretched of places, in which the suffering and pain of humanity dwell. He recounts how, many a time, as the moments of pain became unbearable, he asked himself, "Why was I born a poet and not a shepherd for the sheep or a fig tree on whose branches the birds of the skies can build their nests?"

But whether transcendent or raw, Abdul Samad's feelings were continuously transformed into sensational poems. The poet has published five volumes of Arabic poetry, in which he has taken up a diverse range of topics, including politics, spirituality and love. He has dedicated many poems to the different women who have influenced his life — his mother, his wife, his daughters and his female friends and teachers. "The most beautiful of existence is a woman. Mountains end in summits and oceans in depths but a woman has no end. A woman is the mother, the sister, the daughter, the wife and the lover," the poet states.

At the time of his arrival in the United States, Abdul Samad explains that there was a very wide gap between the East and the West, where there was "no connectedness and no bridges to connect the two civilizations."

He recounts his first encounter with the West. "I left Ras Al Maten carrying in my heart the warmth of my village, the greenness of the pines, the redness of the Mediterranean sunsets and the melodies of the nightingales. When I first arrived in the US, I was deafened by the loud noises of New York City, dizzied by its rapid pace and suffocated by its crowded buildings. I was a stranger amid strangers. At that time, many obstacles stood in the way of Arabs living in the US—an anti-Arab media in all its forms, the unresolved Arab-Israeli conflict and America's agenda behind it, and also the prevalent Orientalist discourse."

The New Pen League

However, despite the obstacles planted in an Arab-American's path at the time, Abdul Samad, along with a group of other Arab-American intellectuals, joined hands and set off on a mission to build bridges between the two civilizations. They specifically concentrated on the realm of literature and arts, for, as put by the poet, "the West needed to be introduced to our stories and poems, ones that spoke of our human experience, and most importantly, ones that were told by native Arab voices and not narrated by Western reporters."

Hence, cultural meetings and social gatherings were held at universities and community venues, which helped in crossing cultural boundaries.

As a result, in an effort to counter the West's negative discourse on Arabs, the New Pen League (NPL) was established in 2005 as a secular, non-political and non-profit organization, with a mission to "express cultural literary and artworks of Arab-Americans in the United States."

The NPL was a modern attempt at revisiting and reviving the golden era of Kahlil Gibran of the early 1900s, during which the original Pen League was a source of identity and pride for every Arab living in the West. Today Abdul Samad is the acting dean of the New Pen League.

A Poet and a Chef

In another realm, Abdul Samad happens to be the owner of many restaurants in New York City. "It all started when I realized I was able to touch the hearts of Westerners not only via their eyes and ears but also through their mouths!" he says light-heartedly. And it was on that note that he opened his first 40-square-metre falafel shop in 1971 in a neighborhood adjacent to Columbia University, "at a time when the word falafel was rarely part of the American menu".

"But it was more than just a passion for cooking; it was about building an identity for Arabs in the West. Only a few years later, my tiny shop became a gathering place for Arab students, a haven in which they could reminisce about, smell and taste their homeland."

Abdul Samad's tiny shop has since fathered many other branches on Broadway, ones that were once described by the late Edward Said as "pieces of a homeland."

In the early Nineties, a photo of one of Abdul Samad's branches, Ameer Al Falafel, was hung in a museum of the city located on 105th Street and 5th Avenue as one of the "cultural marks" of New York City. In 1995, Samad Deli (another of the branches) burned down. The heavy-spirited poet arrived the next morning only to find roses and letters at the door of the deli and to later read in *The New York Times* issue of February 11, 1996: "Love letters are not what you expect to find taped to the front door of a waterlogged neighborhood deli. But love letters are what you find stuck to the glass of Samad Deli, on Broadway between 111th and 112th streets, which has been shuttered since a fire shortly before New Year's Day."

Nizar Qabbani's Letter to the Poet

In a letter addressed to Youssef, world-renowned Syrian poet Nizar Qabbani wrote:

London: 20 /3 / 1994

Beloved Youssef,

Your letter was a pleasant surprise, for after your long exile in the country of Walt Disney and McDonalds, I was not expecting your style of writing to be of such radiance and grace.

It has been the habit of those who leave ... [Lebanon] to sell their history and dispose of their language in the "kashah.¹"

But you, dear Youssef, have managed to stay fit, psychologically and linguistically ... And what is most beautiful about you is your poetic memory ...

Has poetry died, as they say?

Perhaps those who savor poetry have died ... perhaps it was killed by Michael Jackson and Madonna, the F-16 fighter jets, and the new world order that insists on transforming us into waiters serving at the table of the one and only master who does not have a partner.

Perhaps the voice of poetry was suffocated, and the only thing that remains for us to listen to is CNN TV ...

Then again, poetry will never be defeated this easily—for as long as there is a man like you who gargles with its water day and night, poetry will forever remain the king of kings.² ...

---

¹ Kashah refers to a basket used by Syrian merchants who immigrated to North and South America years ago and with which they carried and sold merchandise while walking by foot from one place to another.

² A copy of the original letter in Arabic from Nizar Qabbani to Youssef Abdul Samad appears on the facing page. The translation above is only an excerpt of the original letter.

الحبيب يوسف ،

أسعدتني رسالتُك ، وخاجأتني ..

فلم أكُن منتظراً منك بعد منفاك الطويل في بلاد والت ديزني ، وماكدونالد ،
أن تكون أسلوبُك مثل هذا التوهّج والنضارة .

نحن عادة الذين يرحلون عن شارع المعرّض ، وسوق النورية ، وساحة
رياض الصلح ، ووطا المصيطبة ، والمسبغة التحتا .. أن يبيعوا تاريخهم ، ويطرحوا
لغتهم في (الكنسة) ..

أما أنتَ ، يا يوسف ، فلا تزال والحمد الله بكامل لياقتك النفسية
واللغوية .. ولا تزال حاملاً على كتفيك بناية بنك بيروت والبلاد العربية ،
وأيامنا الجميلة فيظ ، حيث كان تناول القهوة معك عند الصباح ، خروجاً
على نظام المصارف .. وتحدياً جميلاً لأرقامهم ، وحساب الودائع ، ودفاتر الشيكات .

أما ذاكرتُك الشعرية ، منِّي أحلى ما فيك ..
فلا تزال (هوامش على دفتر النكسة) تحفظ أعصابك ، ودورتك
الدموية ، كما ظلّت تحرق دورتي الدموية ، حين كتبتُها ..

هل مات الشعر ؟ كما يقولون ...
ربما مات من يذوقون الشعر ، ويحملون أحقادهم به ..
ربما قتله (مايكل جاكسون) .. و(مادونا) .. وطائرات الإف ٦/ ..
والنظام العالمي الجديد .. الذي يريد أن يحولنا إلى غارسونات نخدم
على مائدة السيد الواحد الأحد .. الذي لا شريك له ..

ربما اختنق صوت الشعر .. ولم يبق لدينا ما نسمعه سوى
تلفزيون ال C.N.N. ..

الشعر ، لا يموت مثل هذه السهولة .. وما دام هناك رجل مثلك
تتفجر من دماء الشعر صباح مسا .. فإن الشعر سيبقى ملك الملوك ..
إنني مسافر بعد غد إلى دبي ، وسأغيب عن لندن حوالي أسبوعين ،
وقد أردتُ أن أكتب لك قبل سفري ، لأشكرك على رسالتك الرائعة ،
فشكراً لنور التي أعطتك كل هذه الشفافية ، وحفتك من التلوث
الأميركي ، وقبلاتي إلى الحبيب نزار وأخوتك واحداً واحداً ..
وإلى لقاء قريب في واشنطن بإذن الله .

نزار

A Final Note

Before coming to an end, I would like to extend my sincere appreciation to Professor Mansour Ajami whose opinion on each and every translated poem was of great value, and whose words of encouragement added wood to my fire. Dr. Ajami is a man of great knowledge and expertise in the field of translation. He is a translator/reviser at the United Nations Headquarters in New York and has taught Arabic language, literature and culture at Princeton, Columbia, Berkeley and other major universities in the U.S. and abroad.

Once again, I would like to express my gratitude to the poet Youssef Abdul Samad whose confidence and trust in my translation is what gave birth to this book.

I thank my friends for being my daisies in life's rigid terrains, and, as is in the words of Kahlil Gibran, for "being my needs answered;" a special thank you goes to Cathy Newsome and Anita Savage for lending me their "Western" ears.

I am grateful for my beloved father, Dr. Jabr Al-Atrash, whose footsteps are my trail to success, my mother Faiha for believing in me, and my brothers Gheath and Ghayth for their unconditional love and support.

Lastly, to each member of my precious family I say: you are my suns, moons and stars; you are the meaning of my life.

And it is *so that the poem remains*, so that the young can better understand the old, and so that there is universal harmony and connectedness between East and West, I present my readers with this work of translation.

> *Ghada Alatrash*
> Cranbrook, BC, Canada
> August 2012

So That the Poem Remains

حَتّى تَبقى القصيدة

THE SPIRITUAL

"Poets are masters of us ordinary men, in knowledge of the mind, because they drink at streams which we have not yet made accessible to science."

—Sigmund Freud

And the Poem Remains

"If Earth were to return to water,
to water we would also return,
and the poem remains."

—*Youssef Abdul Samad*

And the Poem Remains

Don't you realize
that I have known you
since before your existence?

And, after the Earth was formed
we came to meet
as was predestined.

I patiently awaited
the slow beginning of time,
and then entered its passage
and travelled
in its eternal body
a thousand times
searching for you,
meanwhile you were next to me.

I asked all women about you
whilst you were all women.
I gazed at you
and savored you,

وَتبقى القصيدةُ

ألا تعلمينَ بأنِّي

عرفتُكِ من قبلُ أن توجدي؟!

ومن بعد أنْ

صارتِ الارضُ جئنا إليها

وكنَّا على موعدِ

توانَيتُ في الزمَنِ المُبتدا

ومنهُ دخلتُ على الموضعِ

وسافرتُ في جسَدِ الدهرِ ألفاً

أُفتِّشُ عنكِ وأنتِ معي

وأسألُ عنكِ النساءَ

وأنتِ جميعُ النساء

وأُمعنُ فيكِ وأستمتعُ

and could not break away
from underneath your shade.

I entered your depths,
and scooped from
the depth of your depths,
but I remained unfulfilled,
while you became greener,
more fruitful.

There was no end
to your bread and water,
and the man in me
could not be quenched,
for in you
there is no end to women.

How does your loaf not lessen?
We eat from it
but it does not lessen!

We distance ourselves from you,
we turn away from you,
but after a short while,
we return
desiring more
of your coveted bread.

ومن تحتِ ظلِّكِ لا أطلعُ

وأنزلُ أغرفُ من عُمقِ عمقِكِ

أغرفُ منكِ ولا أشبعُ

ويخضرُّ فيكِ العَطاءُ!

ولا ينتهي منكِ خُبزٌ وماءُ!

ولا رجلُ الارضِ بي يرتوي

ولا تنتهي فيكِ أنتِ النساءُ!!

لماذا رغيفُكِ لا يَنقصُ؟!

ونأكلُ منهُ ولا يَنقصُ!

وننفرُ منكِ، وعنكِ نحيدُ

وبعدَ قليلٍ.. نعودُ

ومن خبزِكِ المُشتهى نَستزيدُ!!

How is it
that while the nights age in us,
you remain untouched;
we wear you throughout the ages,
but like a rose in a poem,
you do not wither;
recited a thousand times,
it always remains new!

If Earth were to return to water,
to water we would also return,
and the poem remains.

لماذا!؟!

وتعتقُ فينا الليالي

وأنتِ تظلِّينَ جدّاً جديدة

ونَلْبَسُكِ العمرَ في كلِّ يومٍ

ولا تذبلينَ كأنَّكِ وردُ القصيدة

نُرَدِّدُها ألفَ دوْرٍ وتبقى جديدة

إذا عادتِ الارضُ ماءًً..!

نعودُ إلى الماءِ نحنُ ... وتبقى القصيدة.

God Is Knowledge

"Many 'religious' people are stuck at that level.
They equate truth with thought,
and as they are completely identified with thought (their mind),
they claim to be in sole possession of the truth
in an unconscious attempt to protect their identity."

—*Eckhart Tolle*

God is Knowledge

To those who place on the scale

what they are ignorant of

and who work as merchants for God's religions,

carrying the Book of God

in their hands,

and insist on judging others while they are devoid of all reason;

who see but lifeless letters

in the context

and do not allow for progress and evolution—

To them, I say:

God does not end in His beginning,

so how can you end Him in "Be or become?"[3]

God is His verses

and God is knowledge,

and those who confine His meaning have gone astray.

---

[3] The poet is referring to Surat "Ya Sin" in *The Holy Koran* (Chapter 36, verse 82): "In fact, when he intends a thing, His command is: 'Be'—and it becomes."

يا مَن يحطُّونَ في الميزانِ مَنْ جهلوا

ويعملونَ لدينِ اللهِ تُجَّارا

ويحملونَ كتابَ اللهِ في يدِهمْ

ويحكمون بغيرِ العقلِ إصرارا

يرونَ في النصِّ حرفاً لا حياةَ بهِ

ولا يُقيمون للتجديدِ مِعيارا

واللهُ لا تنتهي فيهِ بدايتُهُ

فكيفَ تُنهونهُ في كانَ أوْ صارا؟!

أللهُ.. آياتُهُ واللهُ معرفةٌ

ومنْ يحدِّدُ معناهُ فقد وارى

For He has been in humans since eternity,

long before religions

acted as our magnifying glasses.

I stood in awe

in the midst of His wonder,

and I gazed upon Earth and extracted its underlying mysteries,

and it was only His order

that could be seen,

one of godliness and of mercy.

For in death and in life

and all that is related,

God remains the essence of all.

I stood dumbfounded

at the harm and injuries

that my hands have left behind on Earth,

at what my feet had trod upon

of what was once pure

and later polluted by Cain's hands for ages to come.

Perhaps my failure, my squandering,

and the murder of my people

were the driving force behind my revolutionary scream.[4]

---

[4] The poet is referring here to his controversial poem *Return the Hoopoe to Us,* one that stirred religious debate and disagreement.

وكانَ في داخلِ الانسانِ من أزَلٍ
من قبل أن جعلَ الادِيانَ مِنظارا

وعندما ارتبتُ في السِّرِّ المُحاطِ بهِ
نظرتُ في الارضِ واستخرجتُ أسرارا

وما وجدتُ لغير اللهِ منزلةً
ولمْ أجدْ غيرَه ربّاً وغفَّارا

فالموتُ والعيشُ والجيرانُ كلُّهمُ
اللهُ أقربُهم، مهما دَنَوا جارا

لكنني بعدما أبصرتُ ما تَرَكتْ
يدايَ في الارضِ إضراراً وأضرارا

وقدْ خطَوتُ عليها بعدما غُسِلتْ
ولوَّثتها يدا «قايين» أدهارا

لعلَّهُ كانَ إخفاقي وبعثرتي
وقتلُ أهلي الذي في صرختي ثارا

I saw my homeland
drenched in blood
as they spilled rivers of fires on its grounds.

We returned as sinners
without punishment,
but were no longer considered by the Book of Wisdom as pious.

I distanced what belonged to God on Earth
so that all of what remained
could be destroyed,

just as God had distanced Lot[5]
from his inhabited world
in order to wash away human sin.

I released a hoopoe[6] that was caged in our blood
so that he may return with what was bestowed upon him
when he first began to fly.

I stoked the fire,
so that we may be renewed
and re-emerge as pure and noble.

---

[5] Lot is Abraham's nephew who was warned to leave from Sodom and Gomorrah before the destruction of the city.

[6] From the poem *Return the Hoopoe to Us* where the hoopoe is the deliverer of the truth that could not be announced except in the land of freedom, and not under the conditions of pressure and terror.

وقد رأيتُ بلادي في الدماءِ وهمْ

يكَبْكِبونَ عليها النارَ أنهارا

ونحنُ عدنا خطاةً لا عقابَ لنا

ولمْ نعدْ بكتابِ العقلِ أبرارا

أبعدتُ عن أرضِهِ ما لمْ يكنْ عَدَماً

لكنْ يُبَدَّدَ ما للناسِ وانهارا

كأبعدَ اللهُ «لوطاً» عن عمورتِهِ

وراحَ يغسلُها كي يغسلَ العارا

طيَّرتُ هذْهُدَه المقفوصَ في دمنا

لكي يعودَ بما أُوتي متى طارا

ورحتُ للنارِ أُذكيها لِتُبْدلنا

ونُسْتَرَدَّ أثيريِّين أطهارا

I prayed for the winds
to storm the people
with their thunder and rain,

and to bring them out of
the darkness of their graves
just as the earth blossoms with flowers after death.

As a result, they called me a pagan,
and they believed in their ignorance
that my language is renunciation.

So, I went on re-examining and retracing,
but I couldn't find,
other than for God, any traces.

Praise him who says
that people's religions are their personal choice,
for we were created on Earth time and time again.[7]

God is immense knowledge,
and he who is ignorant of it will live in fire
even when he dwells not in fire.

And he who sees
there is only one road home
and cannot see another, will not enter.

---

[7] The poet is here referring to Surat "Nuh" (Noah) in *The Holy Koran* (Chapter 71, verse 14).

دعوتُ مؤتَفكاتِ الريحِ تضربهمْ

وتملأُ الناسَ إرعاداً وإمطارا

وبعدَها من ظلامِ القبرِ يُخرجهمْ

والارضُ تُخرجُ بعد الموتِ أزهارا

فكفَّروني وظنّوا أنَّ في لُغَتي

من جهلهمْ لوجودِ اللهِ إنكارا

فعدتُ أقرأها مثنى وأعرفها

وما وجدتُ لغير اللهِ آثارا

سبحانَ من قال دينُ الناسِ ملكُهمْ

وقدْ خلقناكمُ في الارضِ أطوارا

اللهُ معرفةٌ كبرى وجاهلُها

يعيشُ في النارِ إنْ لمْ يسكنِ النارا

ومنْ رأى أنَّ دربَ الدارِ واحدةٌ

وما رأى غيرَها لنْ يدخلَ الدارا

My roads to Him are numerous,

and the greater comfort dwells in the heart

of those who are walking.

I reply with "Salam"[8]

to all who can speak,

but they pay no heed to what I say.

It is only when you journey

to your innermost being

that my words are justified.

Search,

for you are bound to find if you search,

and God will certainly not deal with a confused heart unjustly.

My religion is mine,

and the religion of humans is theirs;

Praise Him who gives choices to humans and they choose.

---

[8] Salam is the Arabic word for peace, and it also serves as a greeting to one another. The poet is also referring here to Surat "Al Furqân" in *The Holy Koran* (Chapter 25, verse 63): "And the servants of Allah Most Gracious are those who walk on the Earth in humility, and when the ignorant address them, they reply: 'peace!' "

أنا دروبي عديداتٌ معابرُها

إليهِ، والراحةُ الكبرى لمن سارا

إني أُجيبُ: «سلاماً» كلَّ مَنْ نطَقوا

من غيرِما أدركوا ما قلتُ تَكْرارا

ولو رجعتمْ إلى ما في سرائرِكمْ

وجدتمُ للذي أعلنتُ أعذارا

وفتِّشوا تجدوها فتِّشوا تجِدوا

واللهُ لا يُظْلِمُ القلبَ الذي حارا

ديني لنفسي ودينُ العالمينَ لهمْ

سُبحانَ من خيَّرَ العبدَ الذي اختارا

Al-Shqaif Hermitage

"I do not feel obliged to believe that the same
God who has endowed us with sense,
reason and intellect has intended us to forgo their use."

—*Galileo Gelilei*

"Everywhere I go I find that a poet has been there before me."

—*Sigmund Freud*

Al-Shqaif Hermitage[9]

To my village "Ras El Maten," and to the spirit that has triumphed over
soil and conquered it with its defiance and its immortality,
the spirit of the virtuous Sufi leader Kamal Junblat.

My brothers[10], snatch me away from the land of labyrinth
for in it I suffer from two longings;

hold on to the remnants of a village that has remained within me,
and take me back to the trails of my childhood.

The Earth has closed in on me and has worsened in appearance,
for it has been permeated with animalistic greed.

Its water—all of its water—could not cleanse
what has been spoiled by the hands of man.

As the floods around me distend above the waterlines,
I anxiously search for a safe haven.

It is then that my village emerges from behind the places,
in a location higher than that of the floods,

where the soul can escape the tyranny of mankind
and find shelter from the forthcoming darkness.

---

9   A cave formed by nature on a rock that stands at tremendous height. It was converted by a religious
    man to a place of reverence and worship. It also happens to be the place in which Lebanese and Sufi
    leader Kamal Junblat practiced solitude and meditation on a number of occasions.
10 Fouzi and Aref, the two brothers of the poet.

خلوة الشريف

إلى ضيعتي (رأس المتن)،
وإلى الروحِ التي غَالبت الترابَ وغلَبتْهُ
بتمرّدها وخلودها،
روحِ الصوفي الروحاني "كمال جنبلاط"

أخويَّ من أرضِ الضّياعِ خُذاني

فأنا هنا من غربتَيْنِ أعاني

وخذا بقايا ضيعةٍ بقيَتْ معي

وعلى دروبِ طفولتي ردّاني

الارضُ ضاقتْ بي وساءَت منظراً

وطغَتْ عليها نَزوةُ الحيوانِ

والماءُ... كلُّ الماءِ ليسَ بغاسلٍ

ما أفسَدَتْ منها يدُ الانسان

وكأنني والسَيْلُ قدْ غَمرَ الربى

حولي، أفتِّشُ عن مكانِ أمانِ

وتُطِلُّ من خلفِ الاماكن ضيعتي

من موضعٍ يعلو على الطوفانِ

فيها نجاةُ الروحِ من ظُلْمِ الورى

وبها يُلاذُ من الظلامِ الداني

O how I wish to find a cave in her[11] rocks
in which I could live—one with two doors:

a door that overlooks the green meadows
and a second open to the secrets of the soul;

a place to where I could flee, not in escape but in return,
from the superficial to the introspective world;

where I could live on that which could neither be bought, sold,
nor placed on a scale;

where I could drink avidly from a spring of overflowing water,
not from poison-filled bottles;

and where I could live my inert emotions
as if I had been quenched with the water of life.

Ras El Maten[12] will always remain my timeless home on Earth,
one that will keep me from dissolving.

Her water and her greenery are only a few of her promises,
and her springs are a cure for a rusted thirst.

The borders of Ras El Maten are beyond her own borders,
and the destiny of Ras El Maten is the best of destinies.

---

[11] Here, the poet is referring to his home village of Ras El Maten in Lebanon.
[12] The birthplace of the poet in the mountains of Lebanon.

يا ليتَ لي في صخرةٍ من صخرها

كهفاً أعيشُ به لهُ بابانِ

بابٌ على خُضرِ السفوحِ مشرَّعٌ

وعلى خفايا الروحِ بابٌ ثانِ

وأفرُّ لا هَرَباً ولكنْ عودةً

من خارجٍ للعالمِ الجَوّاني

أحيا على ما لا يُباع ويُشترى

أوْ لا (يُحَطُّ) بكفَّة الميزانِ

وأعبُّ من ينبوعِ ماءٍ دافقٍ

لا من سمومٍ عُبِّئتْ بقناني

ولَطالما أحيا مواتَ مشاعري

وكأنَّهُ ماءَ الحياةِ سقاني

وتظلُّ (رأسُ المتنِ) آخرَ منزلٍ

في الارضِ يحفظني من الذوبانِ

الماءُ والخضراءُ بعضُ وعودِها

وعيونُها تَشفي صدى الظمآنِ

وحدودُ (رأسِ المتنِ) خلفَ حدودها

وزمانُ (رأسِ المتنِ) خيرُ زمان

Give Us Back the Hoopoe

"If you have a particular faith or religion, that is good.
But you can survive without it."

—*The Dali Lama*

"My religion is very simple. My religion is kindness."

—*The Dali Lama*

Give Us Back the Hoopoe[13]

Give us back our paganism and take away

all of what is considered praiseworthy;

but whether or not it returns with the truth,

leave the hoopoe with us.

If they bow to the Sun as a God,

then let them bow![14]

It is better for my nation to be one that worships the Sun and fire

than to be a nation whose religion is: to rely upon and to wait.

For the aspiration of my nation,

the love of my nation,

and the dignity of my people

are greater than worshiping scarecrows.

Return to us the pre-Islamic days,

restore what was revealed in stories,

give us back our sins,

---

13 Hoopoes are distinctive birds. They were considered sacred in Ancient Egypt and were depicted
    on the walls of tombs and temples. Hoopoes also appear in *The Koran*, Surah al-Naml (The Ants)
    27:20-22. *The Koran* says that the hoopoe is intelligent, smart, knows and worships his Creator, and
    was a bird that communicated with King Solomon, ruler of Syria and Palestine.

14 The poet is referring to the hoopoe in *The Koran*, Surat al-Naml (The Ants), 27:22-24, in which the
    hoopoe returns to tell King Solomon that he has obtained knowledge of some people worshipping
    the Sun instead of Allah.

أعيدوا لنا وثنيَّتَنا وخذوا

كلَّ ما عُدَّ مجداً

وإنْ عادَ أو لمْ يعدْ بالحقيقةِ

فلْيُتْرَكِ الهُدهدُ

وللشمسِ من دونِ أنْ وحَّدوا

إذا سجدَ القومُ..! فليسجدوا

دعوا أمتي تعبدُ الشمسَ والنارَ

لا أمَّةً دينُها: اتكلوا واقعدوا

لأنَّ طموحَ بلادي

وحبَّ بلادي

وعِزَّةَ أهلِ بلادي

لأعظمُ من فزعٍ نعبدُ

أعيدوا لنا جاهليَّتَنا

استرجعوا القَصَصَ المنزلَهْ

أعيدوا خطيئتَنا

and take away your paths,
crucifixion, Golgotha,
and all of what is sacred ...

Gather it all up,
and give us back our land without any shadows,
and without one spike of wheat.

For, like the goats,
we would rather survive on bare trees
than in your amazing paradise.

Return to us the land
with its face washed off by a bomb,
so that we may rise from underneath our body parts,
while the promise and the rendezvous vanish,

and so that we may abandon a land of ruins,
dispose of the past while our tomorrow remains,
strip off the dress of our fathers,
and rid ourselves of a history that is but a black twilight zone.

For those whose yesterdays live in their tomorrows
are essentially dead before they are born!

وخذوا الدربَ والصلبَ والجُلْجُلَهْ

وأقداسنا..! كلُّها لَمْلِموها

وردُّوا لنا الارضَ لا ظلَّ فيها ولا سنبُلَهْ

فمن شَجرِ الوعرِ نقْتاتُ كالعَنْزِ جوعاً

ولا الجنَّةَ المُذهِلَهْ

أعيدوا لنا الارضَ مغسولةَ الوجهِ بالقنبلَهْ..!

ومنْ تحتِ أشلائنا نصعدُ

وقدْ ذهبَ الوعدُ والموعدُ

ونهجرُ أرضاً خراباً لنا

فيُنهى المضى ويُظلُّ الغدُ

ونخرجُ من ثوبِ آبائنا

وتاريخُهمْ غَبَشٌ أسودُ

ومن عاشَ في غدهمْ أمسُهمْ..!

يموتونَ منْ قبلِ أنْ يولَدوا

The July of Ages

"Since the time of Homer every European, in what he could say about the Orient, was a racist, an imperialist, and almost totally ethnocentric."

—Edward Said

"For the intellectual, the task, I believe, is explicitly to universalize the crisis, to give greater human scope to what a particular race or nation suffered, to associate that experience with the suffering of others."

—Edward Said

إلى
إدوارد سعيد

The July of Ages

(To Edward Said[15])

The journey of a poet
is but

a temporal death
of a seed

and a seasonal absence
of cocoons.

He rolled the rocks
away from the door,

"I remain in the skeleton,
for a master cannot be stolen by a thief.

I am the eyes of a garden
during a winter's slumber.

I am a revolution in the face of death,
against graves and grave diggers.

---

[15] Edward Said (1935–2003) was a Palestinian-American literary theorist and an advocate for Palestinian rights. He is best known for his book *Orientalism* (1978). He was a university professor of English Comparative Literature at Columbia University and a founding figure in post-colonialism.

تموز العصور

إلى
إدوارد سعيد

رحلةُ الشاعرِ

موتٌ زمنيٌّ

في البذورْ

وغِيابٌ موسميٌّ

في الشرانقْ

دحْرِج الصخرَ

عنِ البابِ

أنا ما زلتُ في الهيكلِ

والسيِّدُ لمْ يسرقْهُ سارقْ

وأنا نومٌ شتائيٌّ

كأحداقِ الحدائقْ

ثورةُ الموتِ على القبرِ وحفَّارِ القبورْ

I am the Tammuz[16] of ages.

Each time the earth is dyed
with red anemones,[17]

I wear the Kermes[18] as a dress
woven with wounds and lilies.

My wounds are like poppies
from which my words are plucked,

The pain of each letter
continues to bleed within me,

and that which bleeds from the waist of the word
is the ink of my pen.

My words are my path to Golgotha[19]
for crucifixion is every poet's destiny.

My body is the bread
broken by a gluttonous earth,
and my blood is the water
distributed at Qana Al Jaleel[20]

My path is pain—

---

[16] Tammuz, Akkadian Dumuzi, in Mesopotamian religion, is the god of fertility embodying the powers of nature's new life in the spring.

[17] Red poppy anemones are known in Arabic as Shaqa'iq An-Nu'man and happen to be common flowers of the springtime season in Middle Eastern regions.

[18] Kermeses are the dried bodies of the female kermes insects, coccus ilicis, which yield a red dyestuff.

[19] Golgotha or Calvary, place of the Skull, is the place in ancient Jerusalem at which the crucifixion of Jesus is said to have occurred.

[20] Qana al Jaleel, also known in English as Cana of Galilee, is a village in Southern Lebanon believed to be the place where Jesus performed his first public miracle and turned a large quantity of water into wine at a wedding feast (John 2:1-11).

أنا تموزُ العصورْ

كلّما خُضِّبَت الارضُ

بأزهارِ الشقائقْ

ألبَسُ القرمزَ ثوباً

من جراحٍ وزنابقْ

وجراحي كالشقائقْ

لمْ تزلْ تُقْطَفُ منها

كلماتي

وَجعُ الحرفِ نزيفٌ داخليُّ

والذي ينزفُ منْ خاصرةِ الكلمةِ

حبرٌ بشريٌّ

أحرفي رافعةٌ جُلجُلتي

والموتُ للشاعر أمرٌ قَدَريُّ

جسدي الخبزُ الذي تكسرهُ

الارضُ الاكولْ

ودمي الماءُ الذي وُزِّعَ

في "قانا الجليلْ"

وطريقي الالمُ، الدربُ

a trail to restful slumber.

My cross is becoming greener
within me,

while I remain, the same,
in all the letters of the words,

and the red dots over the wounded letters
are the nails in the lines.

Whether or not the rocks are rolled away from the grave,
I refuse to enter death,

for between the letter and the wound
are endless revolving conversations.

My life does not stop
at the end of the line.

My journey stretches on,
beyond the letter and the wound,

throughout the ages,
for I am the Tammuz of ages."

إلى النومِ الجميلْ

وصليبي لمْ يزلْ

يخضرُّ في ذاتي

أنا ما زلتُ

في كلِّ حروفِ السطرِ ذاتي

والنقاطُ الحمرُ فوقَ الاحرفِ الكلمى

مساميرُ السطورْ

وإذا دُحرجَ

أو ما دُحْرِجَ الصخرُ عن القبرِ

أنا لنْ أدخلَ الموتَ

وبينَ الحرفِ والجرحِ أحاديثٌ تدورْ

إنَّها لا تنتهي في آخرِ السطرِ

حياتي

رحلتي تمتدُّ

خلفَ الحرفِ والجرحِ

إلى كلِّ العصورْ

أنا... تموزُ العصورْ

THE POLITICAL

The Security Council

"Russia and China have vetoed a European-backed UN Security Council resolution that threatened sanctions against the Syrian regime if it did not immediately halt its military crackdown against civilians. The resolution would have been the first such legally binding move adopted by the Security Council since President Bashar Assad's military began using tanks and soldiers against protesters in mid-March. The UN estimates there have been more than 2,700 deaths."

—*The New York Times*, February 4, 2012

The Security Council

(Written after the Catastrophe of Qana[21])

Beirut!

Has a year

ever passed

without catastrophes,

prisons,

hunger,

and fatigue?

Not a year has lapsed

without a storm,

for it seems like

our destiny is

re-crucifixion

for no reason!

Not a year has lapsed

without the destruction

of our frontlines,

yet our faith

seems to strengthen

with each blow!

---

[21] The 1996 shelling of Qana took place on April 18, 1996 near Qana, a village in Southern Lebanon, in which Israeli defence forces shelled a United Nations compound in which 800 Lebanese civilians had taken refuge. 106 were killed and around 116 injured. A United Nations investigation later determined it was unlikely that the Israeli shelling was a technical or procedural error.

Translation by Ghada Alatrash

مجلس الأمن

بيروتُ..! هَلْ سَنَةٌ مَرَّتْ بلا خُطُبِ

بلا سجونٍ بلا جوعٍ بلا تَعَبِ؟!

ما مرَّ عامٌ ولمْ يَعْصِفْ بنا قَدَرٌ

فنحنُ أقدارُنا صَلْبٌ بلا سَبَبِ

ما مرَّ عامٌ ولَمْ تُضْرَبْ طلائعُنا

ونحنُ نزْدادُ ايماناً على النُّوَبِ

What shall I
leave behind
in my books
for the coming generations
when my present
is a black stain
that has not yet been erased.

Shall I call
on the dead
in their graves
to fight
a war of fire
with canes?

Or shall I
bring back
decayed armies
to return
the land of Arabs
to Arabs?[22]

Do not ask,
"Why do you revolt
with such revenge?"
—It is because
they cast
my family
on the roads,

---

[22] The poet is referring here to two different stories, one found in *The Holy Koran*: Surat al Baqarah
verse 259, and the other in *The Holy Bible*: Ezekiel 37 "The Valley of Dry Bones," verses 1-14.

ماذا سأتركُ للآتينَ في كُتُبي
وحاضري نقْطةٌ سوداءَ لَمْ تَذُبِ

هلْ أستَحِثُّ رجالاً في حفائرِها
حتَّى تحارِبَ حربَ النارِ بالقَصَبِ؟

أمْ أستعيدُ جيوشاً أصبَحَتْ رِمَماً
لكي تُعيدَ بلادَ العُرْبِ للْعَرَبِ؟

لا تسألوني لماذا ثُرتُ مُنْتَقِماً
لأنَّهمْ نَشَروا أهلي على الدُرُبِ

and because
they deprived
my daughter
of her childhood,
and they drowned
all of what was once built
under their flames.

And,
because
they stripped off
the God
they had crucified
and disfigured
the golden mouth
of Yohanna.[23]

By God!
I believe
in the wasteland,
even when
its homes—
the homes of God's soldiers—
lie in ruins.

They told us:
"There is a court
in New York
through which
the rights of land
are returned
to their rightful owners.

---

[23] The Arabic name for John the Golden Mouth, Archbishop of Constantinople and an important
     Early Church Father known for his eloquence in preaching and public speaking.

لأنَّهمْ حَرَموا بنتي طفولتَها

وغرَّقوا ما بنى البانونَ في اللَهَبِ

لأنَّهمْ سَلَبوا الرَّبَّ الذي صَلَبوا

وشوَّهوا فمَ يوحنَّا فَمِ الذَهَبِ

آمنْتُ واللَّهِ بالارضِ الخرَابِ إذا

صارتْ جميعُ بيوتِ الناسِ مِنْ خِرَبٍ

☙

قالوا لنا إنَّ في «نيويورك» محكَمَةً

بها تُعادُ حقوقُ الأرضِ للنُّصُبِ

They said,
"The nations of the U.N.
and their Security Council
are the only ones
who are able
to bring about
such wonders.

"For the Security Council
is a teacher
who instructs nations
on ethics."

Yet,
most nations
with power
remain unethical!

Indeed,
the Security Council
claims,
with its lips,
that the topic
is "under dialogue."

But it gestures a Veto
with its hands—
hands that have proven
good for nothing
but to pull ears
and tails!

ووحدَها أُمَمُ (اليوأنِّ) قادرةٌ

(بمجلسِ الامن) أنْ تأتيكَ بالعَجَبِ

في (مجلسِ الامنِ) أستاذٌ تؤدِّبُنا

ومُعظمُ الدوَلِ العُظمى بلا أَدَبِ

الامرُ مِنْ فمِها شُورى وفي يدِها

(الفيتو) يدانِ لِشَدِّ الأُذنِ والذنَبِ

It walks all over us,
and it walks
in our funeral,
for we are but toys
in its playground.

Yet
if a gnat
simply hovers
in the skies of Haim,[24]
the armies
of the West
impetuously approach us
in anger!

Then,
once we are swallowed
by their flames,
they laugh in secret,
finding blame
and
pronouncing condemnations.

O Security Council,
you are but fire
pointed at the weak
and a face
made of wood!

If Jerusalem,
after the crucifixion,
has become our guiding light,

تمشي علينا..! وتمشي في جنازَتِنا

فنحنُ في ملعبِ (اليوأنِّ) كاللُّعَبِ

وإِنْ تُحِمْ في سما (حاييمَ) برغشةٌ

طارتْ إلينا جنودُ الغرْبِ في غَضَبِ

ونحنُ إنْ أكَلَتْنا نارُهم ضَحِكوا

في سرِّهمْ واكْتَفوا باللَوْمِ والعَتَبِ

يا مجلِسَ الامنِ يا ناراً مُوَّجَهَةً

إلى الضعيفِ ويا وَجْهاً مِنَ الخَشَبِ

إنْ صارتِ القدسُ بعد الصَلْبِ قِبْلَتَنا

then the sand of Qana,
on which a thousand prophets have risen,
becomes our holiest!

My Country speaks love,
but its cedar branches
refuse to kneel
on their knees.

It shall not
rush to sign submissively,
and it does not believe
that the fruits of victory
could be won by escaping.

By God!
Let not
our history bow,
even if it were
for an era of gold!

I bless
a yesterday
that illuminated
and passed by
with honour,
and soared beyond
the summits
of ages and decades.

فأرضُ (قانا) علَيْها مرَّ ألفُ نبيْ

أنا بلادي كلامُ الحُبِّ مَنْطِقُها
وأغصُنُ الارْزِ لا تجثو على الرُّكَبِ

ولا تطيرُ إلى التَوْقيعِ صاغرَةً
ولا ترى ثَمَرَاتِ النصْرِ في الهَرَبِ

باللهِ .. لا تَجعَلوا التاريخَ مُتَّكَأً
حتَّى ولو كانَ ذاكَ العصرُ مِنْ ذَهَبِ

إنِّي أُبارِكُهُ عصْراً أتى ومضى
مشرَّفاً فوقَ هامِ الدَّهرِ والحِقَبِ

I hang its photo
as a medal of distinction,
and as colorful embellishment
on my domes.

Yet again, I am left
without a home
in which I could seek refuge,
and without a fountain
from which my thirst
could be quenched.

Today we stand
on the threshold of a battle,
and it is
only knowledge
that separates
seriousness
from playfulness.

For if the sword
of my knowledge
does not protect me,
then I will surrender the matter
to chaos and disorder.

The buried troops
will not return
my glory,
nor can the sword
of my father
free my children.

أحبُّهُ صورةً خلفي أُعَلِّقُها
وزينةً تكْتَسي أَلْوانَها قِبَبِي

لا مَنْزِلاً كلَّما شُرِّدْتُ أُنْزَلُهُ
أوْ مِنْهَلاً ترتوي مِنْ مائِهِ قِرَبِي

اليومَ نحنُ على أبوابِ مَعْرَكَةٍ
والعِلْمُ يَفْصِلُ بينَ الجِدِّ واللَّعِبِ

إنْ لمْ يَذُدْ عن كياني حدُّ مَعْرِفَتي
وأُرْخِيَ الامرُ للفَوْضى وللشَغَبِ

ولَنْ تُرَجِّعَ مجدي فِرْقَةٌ دُثِرَتْ
ولنْ تُحَرِّرَ أبنائي سيوفُ أبي

By God!
It's not history
that is my lineage,
but today and tomorrow
are my history.

We must
shred all books
of the dead,
and we must
cease to mention
the names
of those deceased.

Indeed,
"Hitteen,"[25]
and Salah ad-Din's[26] steed
were once,
but they are now
with the dead
under ground.

The war of existence
is the only war
that remains,
and a moment of glory
undrapes
the darkness of doubts.

There,
history
is studied
in books,
but here
we see the making of history
in close proximity.

---

[25] The battlefield in Palestine where Muslims and Crusaders fought.
[26] Known in the West as Saladin; a famous Muslim commander (1138–1193), who became the first Sultan of Egypt and Syria and founded the Ayyubid Dynasty. He is also a celebrated example of chivalry principles.

تَاللهِ .. لا تَجعلوا التاريخَ لي حَسَباً

فاليومُ والغَدُ من عُمري هما حَسَبي

ومَزَّقوا كُتُبَ المَوتى بِرُمَّتِها

واستأصِلوا ذِكرَ مَنْ ماتوا.. مِنَ الكُتُبِ

(حطِّينُ)..؟ خيلُ (صلاحِ الدينِ)..؟ أَخيلَةٌ

بَدَتْ وبادَتْ معَ الامواتِ في التُّرَبِ

حربُ البقاءِ هي الحربُ التي بَقِيَتْ

ووقْفَةُ العِزِّ تجلو عَتْمَةَ الرِيَبِ

هناكَ..؟ يُسْتَحْضَرُ التاريخُ مِنْ كُتُبٍ

وها هنا نُبْصِرُ التاريخَ عَنْ كَثَبِ

New York After the Storm

"When I despair, I remember that all through history, the way of truth and love has always won. There have been tyrants and murderers, and for a time they seem invincible, but in the end, they always fall. Think of it, always."

—*Mahatma Ghandi*

New York After the Storm

O New York, your white smile has turned yellow;
is it love that has turned you this transparent,
or have you come down with a sickness, my darling?

New York…
You are forever a piece of my eternity,
and not even sleep could obscure you from my eyesight.

Countless are the memories between us,
ones that are fragrant
with the most delightful of aromas.

Was it old age that led you to give up and surrender
to an earthquake in despair,
or was it a catastrophe that dethroned your two towers?

As I gaze at you today,
I am very saddened not to see them;
but perhaps it is my love for you that has blinded me.

I look for their shadows in frenzy,
and I become horror-struck
when I don't see a trace of them.

نيويورك بعد العاصفة

(نيويوركُ) ضحكتُكِ البيضاءُ صفراءُ

هلْ شفَّكِ الوجدُ أمْ أودى بكِ الداءُ؟

(نيويوركُ) قِطعةُ خُلْدٍ أنتِ في خَلَدي

وليسَ يمحوكِ من عينَيَّ إغفاءُ

بيني وبينكِ، مما كانَ من ذِكَرٍ

تضوعُ بالطيبِ، أشياءٌ وأشياءُ

هلْ شاختِ الأرضُ حتى زُلْزِلتْ زهقاً

زلزالَها، أمْ دَهَتْ بُرْجَيْكِ دَهياءُ

إذا نظرتُ إليكِ اليومَ يُحزنُني

أنْ لا أراكِ، فعينُ الحبِّ عمياءُ

أُديرُ طرفي مراراً في مكانهما

ولا أرى لهما ظلاًّ فأستاءُ

My heart rebuts what my eyes see,
and they act as if
they had become worst enemies today.

Can it really be
that the two towers have vanished from my sight,
while the water is still clinging onto their shadows?

Is it possible that
the two wonders are now hidden
after they were once two phoenixes?

It seems as if everything now tastes of salt,
while all tongues of confession
have become mute.

I avert my eyes to cry
but my nausea
keeps my tears from falling,

and sadness fills my soul
just as the space of the blue domes
is now filled with darkness.

ولا يُصدّقُ قلبي ما يرى نظري

كأنَّ عيني وقلبي اليومَ أعداءُ

هلْ تختفي صوَرُ البُرجَيْنِ عنْ بصَري

وقد تشبّثَ في ظلَّيْهِما الماءُ؟

والمستحيلاتُ هلْ تَخفى على أحدٍ

وكلُّ واحدةٍ منهنَّ عنقاء

كأنَّ في فمنا الاشياءَ مالحةٌ

طعماً، وألسنةَ الإفصاح خرساءُ

أغضُّ طرفي لكي أبكي، ويمنعني

عن البُكا، عند غضِّ الطرفِ إعياءُ

ويملأُ الحزنُ روحي مثلما ملأت

مساحةَ القبّةِ الزرقاءِ ظَلماءُ

After the Murder of My Brother

A poem for Palestinian poet Mahmoud Darwish was inspired
by the story of Joseph in *The Holy Bible*.
In his poems, Darwish writes on Youssef
(the Arabic name for Joseph):

"My father, I am Youssef.
O Father, my brothers do not love me,
…they threw me into the well
and accused the wolf,
but the wolf is more merciful than my brothers."

After the Murder of My Brother[27]

After the murder
of my brother,
my cavernous thirst
longs for more blood.

For I am the son of
Adam and Eve,
and a brother
to Abel whom I killed.

I was told that we were
brothers and friends,
but I said, "Better truthful friend
than no friend."

For we survive
on the flesh of our victims
and words are unable
to express our tyranny.

Earth is our mother
whom we have destructively tortured,
whilst she has remained
the compassionate all-merciful.

---

[27] *This poem was written in light of the 2011 Arab revolutions and was specifically inspired by the events that took place in Syria's Friday April 22, 2011 protest, one in which more than 100 Syrian protestors were murdered.*

بعدَ قتلي أخي ظمآئي العميقُ

لمَزيدٍ من الدماءِ يتوقُ

وأنا إبنُ آدمٍ وابنُ حوّاءَ

و(هابيلُ) من قَتلتُ شقيقُ

قِيلَ لي: «نحنُ إخوةٌ أصدقاءٌ»

قلتُ : «نِعْمَ الصديقُ واللاصديقُ»

نحنُ نحيا على لحومِ ضحايانا

وعنْ ظلمِنا الكلامُ يَضيقُ

أمُّنا الارضُ كمْ قَسَونا عليها

بالأَذى والعذابِ وهي الشَفوقُ

As we decay
she carries on,
and so does our wounding
and our slashing of one another.

But why
wreak evil upon one another
when ours is the Earth
and its distant sky?

Peace be upon you
my brother
from the same mother
and the same father!

How is it
that we are unable to come together
when we were once
best companions?

For we are but destined
to one resting place
at which all other roads
will meet.

Is it rational
that we are living in grief,
benumbed and oblivious
to the beauty of existence?

نحنُ نمضي إلى البِلى وهيَ تبقى

فلماذا التجريحُ والتمزيقُ؟

ولماذا أجني عليكَ وتجني؟

ولنا الارضُ والفضاءُ السحيقُ

يا أخي المِنْ أبي وامِّي سلامٌ

كيفَ لا نلتقي وأنتَ الرفيقُ

ولنا من طريقنا مُستَقَرٌّ

واحدٌ، تنتهي إليهِ الطريقُ

أمِنَ العدلِ أن نعيشَ نياماً

عن جمالِ الوجودِ والعيشُ ضيقُ

Christ had risen
after three nights
forgiving of what was inflicted
upon him by a friend.

And, the people of the cave
slept for hundreds of years
but nevertheless
they awakened!

So when will it be
that we shake off our ignorance
and from our slumber
we awaken?

والمسيحُ استفاقَ بعدَ ثلاثٍ

ناسياً ما جنى عليهِ الصديقُ

و»صحابُ الرقيمِ والكهفِ« ناموا

لمئاتِ السنين ثمَّ أُفيقوا

فمتى نحنُ ننفضُ الجهلَ عنَّا؟

ومتى من سباتِنا نستفيقُ؟!

Muntazar's Year

"Freedom is never voluntarily given by the oppressor;
it must be demanded by the oppressed."

—*Martin Luther King*

Muntazar's Year

What can be said of Muntazar[28]
is endless,
for what has been said
is but a short summary
of a sadness
that could not be summarized!

I believe that
all of what has been written,
and all that has been preached,
will remain worthless
because we live in defeat.

If only we can fast from speaking,
and proceed silently in action
until our words
are transformed
into tools in our hands

---

[28] Muntazar al-Zaidi is the Iraqi journalist who shouted at U.S. President George W Bush, "This is a farewell kiss from the Iraqi people, you dog," and then threw his shoes at the president during a press conference on December 14, 2008. On March 12, 2009, he was sentenced to three years in prison for assaulting a foreign head of state during an official visit. On April 7, the sentence was reduced to one year and he was released in September 2009 for good behavior, after serving nine months of the sentence.

Translation by Ghada Alatrash

جميعُ ما نقولُهُ عنْ "منتظَرْ"

لا ينتهي ..

لأنَّهُ المختَصَرُ المُفيدُ

والحزنُ الذي لا يُختَصَرْ

أشعرُ .. أنَّ كلَّ ما نكتبُهُ

وكلَّ ما نَخْطبُهُ

يبقى بغيرِ قيمةْ ..

لأنَّنا نعيشُ في الهزيمَة

لوْ نستطيعُ كلُّنا الصومَ عنِ الكلامْ

ونستمِرُّ صامتينَ عاملينَ

حتى يصبحَ الكلامُ آلَةً بيدِنا

by which we can execute our desires!

It is only then that we should speak again.

How I wish I could become a rose
plucked by the hands of a young Iraqi girl!

How I wish I could become a palm tree
in whose shade
the future ruler of Iraq
can sleep!

If my tears could remedy wounds,
I would have poured them,
and I would have furnished my ribs
for the sake of a hungry child,
and for the sake of a woman crying,
looking for solace in her tears,

and for the sake of a little boy
swimming in his own blood,
begging the sky for mercy,
asking for Muhammad or Jesus,
while it is only
the voice of Moses[29]
that seems to be heard
these days.

---

[29] "Moses" is the English translation for the name "Moussa" in Arabic, and Amr Mohammed Moussa happens to be the Secretary-General of the Arab League, a 22-member forum representing Arab states since June 1, 2001.

تفعلُ ما نريدْ

حينئذٍ .. ننطقُ من جديدْ

هيهاتِ لو أقدرُ أنْ أصيرَ وردةً
تقطفُها صبيَّةٌ من العراقْ

أوْ نخلةً في ظلِّها
.. ينامُ من سيَحكمُ العراقْ

لو تستطيعُ أنْ تبلسِمَ الجراحَ
أدْمُعي ..! ذرَفْتُها ..
وأضْلُعي ..! فرشْتُها
من أجلِ طفلةٍ تجوعْ
وامرأةٍ تبكي ...
وفي الدموعْ
تبحثُ عنْ عزاءْ

من أجلِ طفلٍ سابحٍ في دمِهِ
يسترحمُ السماءَ
تارةً يسألُ عن "محمَّدٍ" وتارةً يسألُ عنْ "يسوغ"
وصوتُ (موسى هذهِ الايامُ).. وحدهُ المسموغ

The shout of Muntazar
is more than just news
transmitted by pens and press,
and much deeper than
a cynical cartoon!

I believe
it is a desperate act
of an enraged man
executed against an oppressor of humans!

Muntazar!
Did he defeat enemies
and liberate women?
Did he raise the earth to the sky?

Was it a last drop of medicine,
a feeling of failure and disappointment?

Or was it
a long awaited scream
that was finally let out
after his patience had surrendered
and committed suicide?

We shall not lose hope,
and we must bear in mind
that it is by patience, learning, and actions,
that dreams are attained.

صرخةُ "منتظرْ" ..!

أكثرُ من خبَرْ

تنقلهُ الاقلامُ والاعلامْ

أعمقُ منْ (كاريكاتورٍ) ساخرٍ

أظنُّها ! مأساةَ كلِّ غاضبٍ ..

بوجهِ ظالمِ البشَرْ

هلْ هزمَ الاعداءْ ؟ .. وحرَّرَ النساءْ ؟

ورفعَ الارضَ إلى السماءِ .. ؟ "منتَظرْ"!

أمْ كانَ ذاكَ آخرَ الدواءِ والشعورَ بالفشَلْ ...

وخِيبةَ الاملْ ؟

أمْ أنَّه ، أمْ أنَّهُ؟

"فشَّةُ خُلقٍ" طالما عاجزُنا انتظرْ

بفارغِ الصبرِ الذي استسلمَ فانتحرْ

وكيفَ تقنطونْ ؟

وصابرُوا والعلمُ والعملْ ..

ثلاثةٌ بهنَّ يُدركُ الاملْ

But after our actions shrank
and after our words ran out,
our soles were transformed into men.

For when souls are oppressed,
heels, teeth and axes are then put to use.

Who will restore our long-standing glory
that was once spread
by our ancestors
and then lost
by our leaders and soldiers
to the hands of destruction?

Who will restore our yesterday
and all that has been stolen
and looted by intruders?

Who will restore the *One Thousand and One Nights*
of Schehrazade[30] in Baghdad
under the palm gazebos,
and on the verandas beneath the Moon?

Muntazar, and two roses,
not a pair of shoes,
thrown in the face of
the ruler of the sky!

---

[30] Scheherazade is a legendary Persian queen and the storyteller of the *One Thousand and One Nights*.

فبعدَ أن تضاءَلتْ فِعالُنا، وفرِغتْ أقوالُنا

تمرجلَتْ نِعالُنا

وحينَ تُظلَمُ النفوسْ !!

تُستَخدمُ النعالُ والاسنانُ والفؤوسْ

أينَ الذي يُعيدُ مجدَنا التليدَ

مما فتح اَلجدودُ ثمَّ ... ضاعْ

وعجزتْ عن ردِّهِ القوَّادُ والجنودُ من يدِ الضياعْ ؟!

أينَ الذي يُعيدُ أمسَنا ،

وما سبا وسلّبَ الدخيلْ ...

والسَهَرَ الطويلْ والانسَ والسمَرْ

في ليلِ "شهرزادَ" .. تحتَ سُعُفِ النخيلِ ..

تحتَ شُرفةِ القَمَرْ ..

"منتظرٌ" ووردتانِ .. لا حذاءْ

رماهما بوجهِ حاكمِ السماءْ..!!

In the opinion of some,

they represent

the paradigm of knowledge,

and the best of

what the media has given birth to,

and the finest of taste

in the art of hospitality.

For when rulers are dwarfed,

and when dreams resign,

our only hope in this life

becomes a shoe.

What is awaited[31] will be born.

Freedom with marvellous order

will come to life,

and it will survive the chaos

that has rotted its people

as decay rots bones.

Peace will be born!

Your excellencies,

the Judges in the Court of God,

I ask you in the name of Hammurabi

who was the first to enact the laws for our humanity,

I beseech you to release Muntazar!

---

[31] The English meaning of the name "Muntazar" is: awaited.

برأي بعضهمْ! يمثِّلون قمّةَ الثقافةْ

وخيرَ ما أنجَبَتِ الصحافةْ

ومنتهى ما وصلَ الذوقُ لهُ في أدبِ الضيافة

ونحنُ من تضاءَلتْ حكَّامُهمْ

ويئسَتتْ أحلامُهمْ

ألمْ يعدْ من أملٍ في هذه الدنيا لهمْ

سوى حِذاءْ ؟!

سيولَدُ المنتظرُ.. الحريةُ البديعةُ النظامْ

من رحمِ الفوضى التي تنخرُ هذا الشعبَ

مثلَ السوسِ في العظامْ ..

ويُولَدُ السلامْ

سعادةَ القضاةِ في محكمةِ القدَرْ

أسألكمْ باسم "حمورابي" الذي شرَّع للبشرْ

أنْ تطلقوا سراحَ "منتظرْ"

You, the People of Great Babylon,
and the builders of the earth
since the oldest of times,
I see Iraq breaking free of chains
and climbing summits once again!

I see...
the clouds after a long exile
returning to Iraq
with rain.

I see the fields becoming green,
the cattle grazing,
and the vineyards
bowing with fruit.

And amazingly,
I see Iraq rise
above its wounds,
tall,
searching the winds and the skies,
looking in the clouds

and

the lightning strikes,
the thunder roars,
and the rain falls.

يا شعبَ بابلَ العظيمْ

ويا بناة الارضِ منذُ الزمنِ القديمْ

أرى العراقَ اليومَ يسحقُ القيودْ

ويكسرُ القمقمَ من جديدْ

أرى الغَمامَ بعدَ هجرِه الطويلِ

عائداً إلى العراق بالمطرْ

وتُعشِبُ الحقولُ ، ثمَّ تُتئمُ الشياهُ ،

ثمَّ تُثقَلُ الكرومْ

وفجأةً !!

أراهُ عالياً على الجراحِ

واقفاً يفتِّشُ السحابْ

يبحثُ في الرياحْ !!

وتَبرقُ السماءُ ...

ثمَّ تُرعدُ السماءُ

ثمَّ يهطلُ المطرْ.

Perhaps If You Returned

In a statement addressed to her homeland of Syria,
Najat Abdul Samad writes in her novel *Lands of Exile*,
"Our pleas have become hoarse;
love us and put an end to our exile!"

Perhaps If You Returned[32]

Perhaps if you returned,

the people would also return to their homes

after a long absence and a crazy civil war.

And perhaps the days of glory

would bring just one day back to me

so that I can hold onto you and never let you go.

Your homes are still awaiting your return

with buds in your rose-beds,

and so is the path to a church

whose bell is pleading, "Ring me."

My eyes are still jealous over your eyes,

and they lack much sleep—O, my poor eyes.

Do you remember the time when we were young

and when the neighbors saw me embracing you,

and our story became everyone's talk,

and the news reached your parents,

and they threatened me,

warned me,

and their enemy they made me.

---

[32] This poem is translated from Lebanese colloquial Arabic.

☙ *Translation by Ghada Alatrash*

بركي انرجعتي بيجو عالدّار أهل الدارْ

من بعد غيبي طويلي وحرب مجنوني

وبركي الزمان المضى من عمرنا بشي نهار

بيرجع ومش تاركك مطرح مبتكوني

بقيتْ بيوت اللكن والورد فيها زرار

ودرب الكنيسي وجرس بيصيح دقوني

وبعدا عيوني على شبابيكم بتغار

ومش عبتذوق الغفا من غيرتي عيوني

بتتذكري! تذكري وقت اللي كنا زغار

لمن غمرتك أهالي الحي شافوني

وكبرت القصا ولأهلك وصّلو الاخبار

وتوعدولي وخفو وشك وعادوني

It has been since then

that I had lost my mind and began to write poetry,

and it was also then

that my insanity led me to burn your letters.

But the letters of your name could not be burned in the fire,

while your fire remained burning in my heart

and underneath my eyelids.

With a stroke of a moonlight's feather

I wrote your name,

and your name and the moonlight

became my religion and creed.

And even now, if you ask for the light of my eye as a souvenir,

not the light of one, but of both my eyes, would be yours.

وجنّيت من يومها وبلّشت قول شعار

وقعّدتْ احرق مكاتيبك من جنوني

وحروف اسمك ما كانت تحترق بالنار

وتظلها النار في قلبي وبجفوني

وبريش ضوِّ القمر اسمك كتبتو وصار

اسمك وضو القمر ممِّلي المسكوني

وبعدك إذا ضو عيني بتطلبي تذكار

مش بس عالعين، عالعينين بتموني

ON WOMEN

To My Mother Who Left Me

"I don't go to read this poem much because
it makes me much more than sad,"
wrote our poet Youssef Abdul Samad.

To My Mother Who Left Me

O Mother,
I have lost
your face!

I have been destined
for loss
since childhood,
and for an expatriation
whose heart
is harder
than rocks!

Ever since
I lost your face,
my vision dimmed in sadness,
yearning for an image
that was the most beautiful of artwork.

I am frightened
of the winds of death,
for when they storm

إلى أمي التي تركتني

ضَيَّعتُ
وجهَكِ يا أُمِّي

أنا قَدَري
الضَياعُ من صِغَري
وغربةٌ قلبُها أقسى من الحَجَرِ

مُذْ غابَ وجهُكِ
عنْ عَيْنَيَّ
عَتَّمَتا
حزناً على صورةٍ
من أجملِ الصورِ

وخفتُ منها
رياحِ الموتِ
إنْ عَصَفَتْ

they steer me
amongst ghosts of people.

Yet despite
the vast distances
that separate us,
you remain
closer to my eyes
than my eyesight.

Put your blouse of life
back on,
and return
what was lost
in the unmindful moments
of my life.

When I say
"Mother,"
my body
is healed
from illness,
my soul
from longing,
and my heart
from sorrow.

تُسيْرُني
بين أشباحٍ من البَشَرِ

تكونُ ما بيننا
الابعادُ
شاسعةً
وأنتِ أدنى
إلى عَيْنَيَّ من نَظَري

ردِّي عَلَيكِ قميصَ العيشِ
وارتجعي
ما ضاعَ في غفلةِ الايامِ
من عُمري

أقولُ: "أُمي"
فيَشفى الجسمُ من سَقَمٍ
والروحُ من غربةٍ
والقلبُ من ضجر

Take me

to her grave

so that I can weep

next to her,

and so that I

can sleep soundly

on her bosom.

Take me

to Ras Al Maten,[33]

to my village,

and rescue me

from the

ravenously

consuming mouth

of expatriation.

Take me to a home

that is about to be forgotten,

and leave me behind

on its rejuvenating balcony

so that I can sleep

in tranquility

under the shade of one of its

buckthorn trees.

---

[33] The birthplace of the poet, Ras El Maten is a town located on the western steep slopes of Mount Lebanon, a region known for its pine trees and panoramic views.

خذوني إلى قبرِها

أنتَحِبْ قربَها

وأغفُ على صدرِها

الغفوةَ الرائعةْ

خذوني إلى "رأسِ متني"

إلى قريتي

من فَمِ الغربةِ

الذئبةِ الجائعةْ

إلى الكادَ أن يُنتَسى بَيتُنا

خلفَ

شُرفتهِ الواسعةْ

أنمْ

هادئ البالِ في الظلِّ

في ظلٍّ عوسجةٍ

فارِعة

How I regret
an age
that I have lost
in deceitful desires!

Take me
to my lost village
to the house of
my mother;

take me,
gently,
like a shadow of a cloud,
so that I do not startle
the dreams of my mother,
and so that I can sleep soundly
on her bosom.

My loss—
its end is my village.

Take me
to my paradise,
to my village,
to my lost paradise!

Translation by Ghada Alatrash

وأندمْ على العمرِ
ضَيَّعتُهُ
في المنى الخادعةْ

خذوني إلى ضَيعتي
الضائعةْ
إلى بيتِ أمِّي

خذوني
لطيفاً
كظلِّ السحابةِ
كي لا
أنفِّرَ
أحلامَ أمي
خذوني إلى قبرِها
أنتَحبْ قربها
وأغفُ على صدرها
الغفوةَ الرائعةْ

ضياعي... نهايتُهُ ضيعتي

خذوني إلى جنَّتي
ضيعتي..
جنَّتي الضائعةْ.

Love, Poetry and Madness

"If this be not love, it is madness, and then it is pardonable."

—*William Shakespeare, A Midsummer's Night Dream*

"Love is a smoke made with the fume of sighs,
Being purged, a fire sparkling in lovers' eyes,
Being vexed, a sea nourished with lovers' tears.
What is it else? A madness most discreet,
A choking gall and a preserving sweet."

—*William Shakespeare, Romeo and Juliet*

Love, Poetry and Madness

Once,
my beloved asked me,
"What do love and poetry
have in common
with madness?"

I thought for a long while,
and then answered,
"Love is madness,
and poetry is madness;
and, all three are
the inspiration for
'Be'—and it becomes."[34]

Poetry without love is not poetry—
it is but chaotic,
rambling gibberish.
Madness in poetry
is the beauty of poetry,
whether or not it rhymes.

---

[34] The poet is referring to Surat "Ya Sin" in *The Holy Koran* (Chapter 36, verse 82): "In fact, when He[God] intends a thing, His command is: 'Be'—and it becomes."

سألتني يوماً ملهمتي:
"ما الجامعُ بين الحبِّ، وبينَ الشعرِ
وبينَ الما ندعوهُ جنون"؟

فكَّرتُ طويلاً ثمَّ أجبتْ:
"ألحبُّ جنونْ...
والشعرُ جنون...
وثلاثتُهنَّ ..! لَهنَّ
ثلاثُ ذواتٍ في إحدى،
منها نستوحي:
"كنْ فيكونْ".

الشعرُ بلا حبٍّ... لا شعرْ،
وكلامٌ في الفوضى مسجونْ
وجنونُ الحبِّ..؟ جميلُ الشعرِ
اللاموزونِ.. أو الموزونْ.

Poetry is lost clouds;
love is hungry snow;
and what is in common between
the snow,
the tears of the clouds,
the thundering of the winds,
the shelling of the thunder,
and the swiftness of the lightning
is what we call:
"madness!"

Then, I wandered off in thought,
and returned to tell her,
"Your love is laden with danger--
It's like sleeping on the surface of the river
and running on the face of the Moon.
Your love is rich with secrets and images,
and with it I have changed
the course of fate."

Poetry is madness,
and the poet
is an inventor,
a revolutionary creature
who remains in the fire until the end,
circling its cores
in utter bewilderment.

الشعرُ هوَ الغيمُ الضائعْ

والحبُّ هو الثلجُ الجائعْ

والشيءُ الجامعُ فيهِ الثلجُ

ودمعُ الغيمِ

وعصفُ الريحِ

وقصفُ الرعدِ

وخطفُ البرقِ معاً... ندعوهُ:

"جنونْ"..!

وذهبتُ بعيداً في التفكيرِ وعدتُ أقولُ لها:

"محفوفٌ حبُّكِ بالخطرِ

كالنومِ على وجهِ النَهَرِ

كالركضِ على سطحِ القَمَرِ

وغنيٌّ حبُّكِ بالاسرارِ وبالصوَرِ

ولأنَّا مملوءانِ بهِ

غيَّرتُ بهِ مجرى القدرِ

الشعرُ جنونٌ..! والشاعرْ

مخلوقٌ خلّاقٌ ثائرْ

يبقى في النارِ إلى الآخِرْ

دوّارٌ حولَ محاورهِ

وأمامَ دوائرهِ حائرْ

Love is peace and surrender;
its eyes sleep on coal,
and its dreams
are the palaces of love.

And love's fire
for a burning soul
is but coldness and peace.

A poet is sculpted with fire;
he is a storm in the eye of the storm,
and my muse of poetry
is a revolutionary
who adores dangers.

Her majesty,
my queen,
was bored
of a man
who does not age with old age.

She was bored
with a child
divided between
trust and jealousy.

الحبُّ سلامٌ واستسلامْ

وعيونٌ فوقَ الجمرِ تنامْ

وقصورُ الحبِّ..؟ هيَ الاحلامْ

والحبُّ لظاهُ على

المهجِ الحرَّى...

بردٌ وسلامْ

والشاعرُ مجبولٌ بالنارْ

إعصارٌ في عينِ الاعصارْ

وأنا ملهمتي ثائرةٌ

تهوى الاخطارْ".

ملَّت مولاتي من رجلٍ

لا يكبرُ في سنِّ الكِبَرِ

برِمَتْ من طفلٍ منقسمٍ

ما بينَ الغَارَ ولمْ يَغَرِ

I am mad about her,

and mad for her,

for she is not of humankind.

I am afraid

to speak of her sweetness

as I might wound

the breeze of dawn.

Her image

remains in my heart,

even after

she had veiled it from my sight.

I gazed at her

as she lit up and faded out,

and I read what was coming.

O how all of time

could be summed up

with her smile

in this brief eternity!

My heart will always long for her,

as it did on that first day it was infatuated with her,

and until the very last day of my life.

وأنا مَنْ جُنَّ بها وَلَهاً

من كانتْ من غيرِ البشَر

وأخافُ بوصفِ عذوبتِها

أن أجرحَ أنسامَ السَحَر

ظلَّتْ في قلبي صورتُها

لمّا حَجَبتُها عن نظَري

ونظرْتُ..!

فضاءَتْ وانطفأْتْ

وقرأتُ خفايا المنتظَر

واختُصِرَ الدهرُ ببسمتِها

في هذا الخُلدِ المُختصَر

وكأوَّلِ يومٍ هامَ بها

سيظلُّ القلبُ يحنُّ لها

ولآخر يومٍ من عُمُري

When Noura is Saddened, the Rain Pours

"If your eyes had not been,
what would the world have been?"

—*Nizar Qabbani*

عندما تَحزن "نورا" يهطل المطر

When Noura[35] is Saddened, the Rain Pours

Was it the sky's dew of the night
that ran down your cheeks,
or was it the light
of the Moon?

Or has the rain
returned to us
and from your eyes
flowed and poured?

Why and how
does the rain come
on a summer's night
from your cloudless eyes?

O my Noura,
do not distrust, for I am your lover,
and yesterday's night
is but a passing shadow.

---

[35] Noura is the name of the poet's wife.

عندما تحزن "نورا" يهطل المطر

أكانَ الذي

أنزَلَتْهُ السماءُ على وجنتَيْكِ

ندى الليلِ

أمْ كانَ ضوءَ القمرْ؟!

أم الغيْثُ عادَ إلينا

ومنْ مقلتَيْكِ هَمَى وانهمَرْ؟

لماذا ومن أينَ في ليلةِ الصيفِ

من صحوِ عينَيْكِ يأتي المطرْ؟

أنورايَ لا تُخطئي إنني

محبُّكِ والامسُ ظلَّ عَبَرْ

Whether you were

or were not,

you remain

in the now and the awaited.

Olga and Lina[36]

stand witness

to our long evenings

of love.

They, who entered our home,

did not steal your treasure,

for they were

the most chaste of humans.

Neither did

their waists

between my hands bend,

nor did their sugar canes break.

Neither did the honeycomb

from her mouth drip

nor did the dress

off her bosoms unveil.[37]

---

36   Olga and Lina are twin women from Vladivostock in far east Russia. They happen to be the poet's
     friends, and they visited him in his home in New Jersey, USA.
37   The poet is referring to both women as one since they happen to be twins.

وأنتِ إذا كنتِ، أوْ لمْ تكوني

تظلِّينَ في الآنِ والمُنتَظَرْ

و"اولغا ولينا" هما الشاهدانِ

على حبِّنا وليالي السمَرْ

ومنْ دخلَ البيتَ لمْ يسرقِ الكنزَ

منكِ وكنّ أعفَّ البَشَرْ

فلا الخضرُ بينَ يديَّ التوى

ولا قَصَبُ السُّكَّرَيْنِ انكسَرْ

ولا الشهدُ نقّطَ عنْ ثغرها

ولا الثوبُ عنْ ناهدَيْها انحسَرْ

We sat
and our love was our fourth,
and my love for you
was like an abbreviated eternity.

We lingered
and our love was our fourth,
and our sleepiness and wakefulness
long lasted.

As we became united in body,
our fatigue retreated,
and we burned our offerings
on the crematory of our blazing passions.

The Earth
spun us together in its rotations
and revealed
that which what was hidden and veiled.

As our souls were exalted
we walked
like apparitions
on water.

جَلَسْنا ورابعُنا حبُّنا

وحبِّي لكِ الابدُ المُخْتَصَرْ

مَكثْنا ورابعُنا حبُّنا

وطالَ بنا نومُنا والسَهَرْ

ولمَّا اتحدْنا بأجسامنا

ولمْ يدنُ منْ مقلتَيْنا الضجَرْ

وضعنا قرابيننا كلَّها

على مَحرقِ الشهوَةِ المُستَعِرْ

ودارتْ بنا الارضُ دوراتِها

وصرنا نرى ما اختفى واستتَرْ

وعدنا سَموْنا بأرواحنا

وسرنا على الماءِ مثلَ الصوَرْ

Yet, whilst our hands
were full of the most appetizing of fruit,
our hunger
could not be quenched.

And,
when we reached our end,
we reaped the harvest,
while the fruit remained in the tree.

وكُدنا من الجوعِ يُودى بنا

وملءُ يدَيْنا شَهيُّ الثَمَرْ

ولمّا بلغنا نهاياتِنا

قطفنا

وظلَّ الجنى في الشجرْ

O Muse of Poetry, Snatch Me Away

"Everyone who masterfully conceals their emotions
explodes like a deluge if they are exposed.
Here I am revealing and writing
about the projection of my heart."

—*Ghada al-Samman*

O Muse of Poetry, Snatch Me Away

O worriless Muse of Poetry,
deliver me from
the torture of sleeplessness!

Snatch me away
before the passing of the years,
before the Sun sets behind the horizons,
and before the fate of death storms the heart,
when to the owner of my soul I must ascend.

Let your love for me
reach the brink of madness
like that of the burning Moon,
so that you can become
that infinite journey for a poet,
beyond the centuries.

❧ *Translation by Ghada Alatrash*

ربّةَ الشعرِ التي فوقَ الظنونْ

خلِّصيني من عذابِ الأرقِ

أدركيني قبلَ أنْ تمضي السنونْ

وتغيبَ الشمسُ خلفَ الافُقِ

قبلَ أن تعصفَ بالقلبِ المنونْ

وإلى مالكِ نفسي أرتقي

وليصلْ حبُّكِ لي حدَّ الجنونْ

كجنونِ القمرِ المحترقِ

كي تكوني في المدى عبرَ القرونْ

رحلةَ الشاعرِ خلفَ المُطلَقِ

And so that you can be the sister
and the passionate mother for my poetry,
after I pronounce my last breath of life.

Pour into my mouth and sad heart,
the oxygen of life
before I drown.

Perhaps if I were to return
from the sea of silence,
we would meet again,
just as we had met once before.

ولشعري الاختَ والامَّ الحنون

بعدَ تسديدي بقايا رمقي

واسكبي في الثغرِ والقلبِ الحزين

أوكسجينَ العيشِ قبلَ الغرقِ

ربَّما إنْ عُدتُ من بحرِ السكونْ

مثلما كنّا التقينا ... نلتقي

And the Question Remains

"How beautiful is, what happened between us;
how beautiful is, what did not happen;
and how beautiful is,
what will not happen."

—*Ahlam Mosteghanemi*

" 'Tis better to have loved and lost / Than never to have loved at all."

—*Alfred Lord Tennyson*

And the Question Remains

And,
on a cold winter night,
one in which
the rain cried
and cried,
I saw you, a phantom,
walking alone,
drenched in rain.
I worried about you
in the cold and frost.
I saw you walking
amidst the raindrops,
like a spot of sunshine
with an image of a body,
walking in between threads
woven by the clouds,
and in between ropes of water
slashing the ruggedness of the mountains
and the nudity of the rocks,
awakening earth's sleeping seeds.
And,
because of how worried I was about you,
I panicked.

وفي ليلةٍ من ليالي الشتاءِ

التي كانَ فيها ...

شتاءٌ كثيرُ البكاءْ

رأيتكِ كالطيفِ وحدكِ تمشينَ

والغيثُ يهمي عليكِ

وخفتُ كثيراً عليكِ ..؟

من البردِ والزمهريزْ..!

رأيتكِ تمشينَ بينَ النقاطِ

كقطعةِ صحوٍ لها صورةُ الجسمِ

تمشينَ بين الخيوطِ التي نَسجتْها الغيومُ

حِبالاً من الماءِ تجلدُ وعرَ الجبالِ وعريَ الصخورْ

وتوقظُ في الارضِ ما قدْ غفا من بذورْ

ومن عُظْمِ خوفي عليكِ اضطربتُ

I tried to break the windows and fly to you,

but I couldn't.

I tried to jump the distances,

but I couldn't carry a body

that had surrendered to sleep.

As my fear intensified,

my heart burned for you,

and my voice choked within my throat.

I feared that I would lose you for eternity.

I tried to cry,

but my eyes were not able to cry.

Quickly,

winter came to an end,

and I was awakened by the chirping of birds.

I began to look for you

in the rugged terrain

and in between the rocks,

but to no avail!

For a shadow cannot be imprisoned,

nor is Earth able to preserve

what was sketched by shades of light.

As I did not find a trace of you,

I became hopelessly sad,

and I asked myself,

"Why do I think of you?

Why am I worried about you?

Why do you remain in the mind?

وحاولتُ خلعَ الشبابيكِ والطيرانَ إليكِ

ولمْ أستطعْ

وحاولتُ قطعَ المسافةِ قفزاً

ولمْ استطعْ

حملَ جسمي الذي كان مستسلماً للرقادْ

ومن شدَّةِ الخوفِ..

قلبي عليكِ احترقْ

وصوتي بداخل صدري اختنقْ

وخفتُ تضيعينَ مني إلى أبدِ الآبدينْ

وحاولتُ أبكي

فلمْ تستطعْ مقلتايَ البكاءْ

وسرعانَ ما مرَّ فصلُ الشتاءِ وزالْ

وتوقظني كركراتُ الطيورْ

وأمضي أفتِّشُ في الوعرِ عنكِ وبينَ الصخورْ

وهلْ يُحبَسُ الظلُّ

أوْ تحفظُ الارضُ ما رَسَمَتْهُ الظلالْ ؟

وحينَ أنا لا أرى أثَراً لكِ

أَحزنُ حتَّى القنوطِ

وأسألُ نفسي :

"لماذا أفكِّرُ فيكِ .. لماذا أخافُ عليكِ ..

لماذا تظلِّينَ في البالْ ؟ !!

And why do I continue to look for you
beyond the borders of thought?"
I killed a thousand whys,
and I asked a thousand questions,
but I could not answer this or that.
What was in the mind,
never left the mind.
For the green traces of your feet
were in stones,
not in sand,
deep rooted,
and only to vanish,
if mountains were to vanish!
After the season of sadness had passed,
nothing, of what was
or of what wasn't
remained,
apart from for those sketches,
and that question.

وعنكِ..؟

أفتِّشُ خلفَ حدودِ الخيالْ ..

وأقتلُ ألفَ لماذا ...

وأسألُ ألفَ سؤال ..؟»

ولا أستطيعُ الإجابةَ عن ذاكَ أو ذا

وما كانَ في البالِ لمْ يبرحِ البالْ

وآثارُ أقدامكِ الخضرِ في الصخرِ لا في الرمالْ

معمَّقةٌ لا تزولنَّ ...ُ حتَّى تزولَ الجبالْ

ومن بعد أنْ مرَّ فصلُ الكآبةِ

لمْ يبقَ من كلِّ ما كانَ أوْ لمْ يكنْ

غيرُ تلكَ الرسومِ...

وذاكَ السؤالْ...

The Art Teacher

"The more I think about it,
the more I realize there is nothing more artistic than to love others."

—*Vincent Van Gogh*

The Art Teacher

Once, my art teacher said to me:
"Draw the moon for us;"
and I replied,
"But I do not trust
the moody³⁸ moon."

So I began to draw grapes
then I plucked them,
puzzled by those who say,
"a bunch of grapes
taste like watered wine!"

I sketched a turtle;
I pencilled in a rabbit;
and I drew a beautiful bird
with feathers colored
like the pupil of an eye.

---

³⁸ By "moody" the poet is referring to the changing and inconstant shape of the moon, in reference to a line from Shakespeare's *Romeo and Juliet*, "O, swear not by the moon, the fickle moon, the inconstant moon, that monthly changes in her circled orb."

قالتْ معلمتي: «صوّرْ لنا قَمَراً»

فقلتُ: «بالقمرِ (الموديِّ) لا أثقُ»

وصرتُ أرسمُ أعناباً وأقطُفُها

مَنْ قالَ عذقُ الدوالي طعمُه مَذِقُ

صوَّرتُ «زلحفةً» كوَّرتُ أرنبةً

رسَمتُ طيراً جميلاً ريشهُ الحَدَقُ

Furious, my teacher demanded:
"Draw the moon for us!"
But instead
a pomegranate appeared,
glittering like the sun.

Outraged, she yelled,
"You failed!"
…O how I long
for a pomegranate
to fall from a branch of our tree!

I thought for long
about her
—my teacher—
on whose breasts
the basil camped.

For I,
I worship pomegranate trees,
under whose shade
I used to sleep
as I felt restless.

ثارتْ معلِّمتي صوَّرْ لنا قَمَراً
فجاءَ رمَّانةً كالشمسِ تأتلقُ

صاحتْ سقطْتَ ومادتْ ليتها سقطتْ
رمَّانتا ذلكَ الغصنِ الذي مشَقوا

فكَّرتُ فيها كثيراً في معلِّمتي
التي على ناهدَيْها خيَّمَ الحَبَقُ

أنا أنا ، شجرُ الرمَّانِ أعبدهُ
كمْ كنتُ في ظلِّهِ أغفو وبي أرَقُ

While I plucked them,
their fire burned me,
and the burn-scars
still remain
after the years.

Once,
I drew a lemon tree
on a piece of paper,
and from its radiance,
the leaves almost budded.

I drew two pomegranates of fire,
and I tasted them—
You who dwell in fire,
believe it when they say
that fire can be such delight.

I still call to mind
their nudity
and I muse over them.
For,
a harvester is lustful.

وكنتُ أقطفهُ والنارُ تُحرقني
وقدْ كبرتُ وظلَّتْ في يدي الحُرَقُ

رسمتُ ليمونةً يوماً على وَرَقٍ
فكادَ منْ ضوئها أنْ يورقَ الورَقُ

صوَّرتُ رمَّانتَيْ نارٍ وذقتُهما
يا ساكنَ النارِ ، طِبْ نفساً ولو صَدقوا

وها أنا لمْ أزلْ أغتابُ عريَهما
وأستعيدُهما، والقاطفُ الشَبَقُ

How is it
that pomegranate seasons
never come to an end,
nor does their
overflowing blood ever burst?

How is it
that they do not gush
while we eat them?
And how is it that
we do not see their fire as they burn?

I confess
that it was I
who plucked that harvest
and bashfully kept it secret,
but steal it, I did not!

فكيفَ لا ينتهي الرمانُ موسِمُهُ

فينا، ولا دمُهُ المهْراقُ يندفقُ

وكيفَ لا يَتفقى حينَ نأكُلُهُ

ولا نرى النارَ منهُ وهوَ يحترقُ

تلكَ القُطوفُ التي خبّأتَها خَجَلاً

أنا مِنَ القَطَفوا منها وما سَرَقوا

When You Awaken

"In your light I learn how to love. In your beauty,
how to make poems.
You dance inside my chest where no one sees you,
but sometimes I do, and that sight becomes this art."

—*Rumi*

When You Awaken

When you awaken
all existence awakens,
and an age that could not be renewed
becomes new.

When you awaken
dawn becomes greener,
hills blossom,
and roses begin to grow.

You are a pleasant dream,
a strange phantom,
and a far away fancy
difficult to attain.

Do not fear
the onset of age
for I will protect you
from ruinous aging.

With the poetry I've written for you
I will help you remain,
for in poetry
everything is renewed.

حينَ تستيقظينِ

حينَ تستيقظينَ يصحو الوجودُ

ويعودُ العمرُ الذي لا يعودُ

حينَ تستيقظينَ يخضوضرُ الفجرُ

وتزهو الربى وتنمو الورودُ

أنتِ حلمٌ عذبٌ وطيفٌ غريبٌ

وخيالٌ صعبُ المنالِ بعيدُ

لا تخافي عليكِ من هجمةِ العمرِ

فانّي أحميكِ ممّا يُبيدُ

وبشعرٍ كتبتُهُ لكِ أُبقيكِ

وبالشعرِ كلُّ شيءٍ جديدُ

How is it
that our beautiful yesterdays
and our sung dreams
came to an end

after all that was shared
of feelings, slogans,
confessions, horizons,
and fantasies?

—back then,
when our dreams were limitless
and our vast horizons
borderless.

But alas, it all faded away
as if it had never been!
What happened to our hopes
and to all the promises?

Tell me,
how are colors and whispers
erased from the mind,
and how does a song die?

Weren't you the spirit
that once found me
as I was a wandering soul
in the void?

إنَّهُ أمسُنا الجميلُ الذي مرَّ

وولَّى، وحلمُنا المنشودُ

يومَ كانتْ لنا المشاعرُ والاشعارُ

والبوحُ والمدى والشرودُ

ولأحلامِنا البعيدةِ آفاقٌ

رِحابٌ... حدودُها اللاحدودُ

وتلاشتْ كأنَّها لمْ تكنْ يوماً...!

فأينَ المنى؟ وأينَ الوعودُ...؟!

أخبريني كيفَ امَّحى اللونُ والصوتُ

من البالِ؟ كيفَ ماتَ النشيدُ؟

أولستِ الروحَ التي اكتشفتني

وانا في الفراغِ روحٌ شَرودُ

Do not be troubled about leaving me,
for ever since I was a child,
I have been alone.

The long nights
have taught me patience
while the thunder
shook my heart.

Leave me to my poetry
and to my writing solitude,
for it is only when I write
that I can bring back what cannot be brought back.

And with what I have written through poetry,
I can preserve what remains of me,
and then, alive,
to dust I will return!

لا تخافي عليَّ أنْ تتركيني
إنَّني منذُ كنتُ طفلاً وحيدُ

وعلى الصبرِ عوَّدتني الليالي
كلَّما هزَّتِ الفؤادَ الرعودُ

أتركيني للشعرِ أكْتبُهُ وحدي
وبِهِ أستعيدُ ما استعيدُ

وبشعرٍ كتبتُ...! أحمي بقاياىَ
وحيّاً إلى الترابِ أعودُ

The Night Became Still

"The night became still / and it is in the stillness
of the night that dreams hide away."

—*Kahlil Gibran*

The Night Became Still

The night became still[39]
and the carefree are asleep,
but those who haven't slept
are an impassioned love and I.

Complaining to one another
of our wounds,
and neither can be blamed
for their complaints.

Upon your visits,
darkness turned into light,
and as you left
light became darkness.

In my bosom
dwells a heart
that overflows with
fragrant feelings and salaam.[40]

---

[39] "The night became still" is borrowed from the opening verse of Kahlil Gibran's poem *The Night Became Still.*

[40] Salaam has two meanings in Arabic: greetings / peace.

سكنَ الليلُ والخليّونَ ناموا

والذي لمْ ينَمْ أنا والغرامُ

نتشاكى ممّا بنا مِنْ جراحٍ

وكلانا إذا اشتكى لا يُلامُ

كنتِ تأتينَ والظلامُ نهارٌ

وتعودينَ والنهارُ ظلامُ

وبصدري ممّا يَفيضُ بهِ القلبُ

شعورٌ معطَّرٌ وسلامُ

"Only if the full moon were to leave its orbit,
my enchanted heart will leave yours,"
—that's what you once said.
But alas! To where have your words gone?

For the moon
still circles in its orbit,
while the pain
still remains in the heart.

How were you able to enslave a soul
that has not for once
been enslaved
by Soha or Sihaam[41]?

My sleeplessness
both kills
and revives me
in endless dreams.

I have become troubled
by her spirit
and troubled about it—
a spirit that was once an inspiration.

Woe unto me,
a thousand times,
and woe unto her,
she who does not fade away nor sleeps!

---

[41] Soha and Siham are female names randomly chosen by the poet.

«إنْ يغادرْ مدارَهُ القمَرُ البدرُ

يغادرُكَ قلبيَ المستهامُ»

هكذا قلتِ لي: ومرَّتْ سُوَيعاتٌ

على القولِ أينَ صارَ الكلامُ؟!

لمْ يزلْ في مدارِهِ القمَرُ البدرُ

وفي القلبِ ظلَّت الآلامُ

كيفَ تيَّمتِ روحَ من لمْ تُتَيِّمْه

ولو مرَّةً...! «سُهى» أوْ «سهامُ»

سَهَري قاتلٌ ومُحيٍ معاً في

لَحظاتٍ كأنَّها الاحلامُ

صرتُ أخشى منهُ وأخشى عليهِ

طيفِ منْ كانَ طيفَها الالهامُ

ألفُ ويلي منهُ وويلي عليهِ

... ذلكَ اللايغيبُ واللاينامُ

More Than "I Love You"

"At the touch of love
everyone becomes a poet."

—*Plato*

More Than "I Love You"[42]

—more than "I love you,"
for "I love you" is not enough,
nor is it able
to extinguish
the fire
burning in your heart.

Nor is "I love you"
able to soothe
the fire of
a flamed "aaah"
that is searing
in your heart and mine.

"I love you" is a sound;
it is like thunder,
for by the time
it shakes the universe,
its rumble vanishes
within the blink of an eye.

---

[42] This poem is translated from Lebanese colloquial Arabic.

أكثَرْ مِنِ بْحِبَّكْ

بحبَّكْ ما بِتْكَفِّي!!

كِلْمِةْ بحبَّكْ وحدها مش قادري

النار البِصدرك شاعلي تطفِّي

ولا قادري "بحبِّك" الآه الشاعلي

بقلبك وقلبي نارها تطفِّي

كلمة بحبك صوتْ متل الرعدْ

ما بيلْحَقِ يهزِّ الدني

تا بعد رمشةْ عَيْنْ صوتو يختفي

"I love you" is a flicker;
it is like lightening,
for by the time
it lights up the sky
its light extinguishes
with the bat of an eye.

I wish a thousand times,
and a thousand times more,
to find in silence
a word whose letters
are not spoken
nor written,

and to practice saying it
and not saying it
until my tongue becomes weary,
while neither of us
happens to know
the word we are looking for.

Yet what I do know
is that we will ultimately
depart this world
without the word we were looking for,
as all the letters of the alphabet
will eventually run out before finding it.

كلمة بحبِّك ضو

متل ومض البرقْ

ما بيلحق يضوِّي السما

تا بعد غمضة عينْ

ضُوُّو ينطفي

يا ريتني ويا الف رَيْتْ

بلاقي شو كلمي حروفها

لا بتنحكى ولا بتنكتب

وظلْ حاول قولها وما قولها

تا يحل علساني التعبْ

وانتِ معي تتسمعي وما تسمعي

ولا أعرف ولا تعرفي

الكلمي اللي مَنَّا نقولها

ونفل من دور الدني

وما نقدر الكلمي اللي منا نحكيا ما نحكيا

ومن بعدنا ...

تخلص حروف المعرفي

وما نلاقيا..!

Hermitage of the Soul

"To love another person is to see the face of God."

—*Victor Hugo*

Hermitage of the Soul

I found you
in the midst of reality and fancy
for you are neither of flesh
nor of fantasy.

You are not a woman
like other women
for you are of light
and they are of darkness.

Your image is sketched
in the form of a shadow,
one that exceeds the scope of my understanding
and surpasses my knowledge.

But how is it that
you come to meet me,
when you are beyond form,
shape, and color?

⚯ *Translation by Ghada Alatrash*

وجدتُكِ ما بينَ الحقيقةِ والوهمِ

فلا أنتِ منْ إنسٍ ولا أنتِ منْ حلمِ

وَلَستِ كإحداهُنَّ مَنْ هُنَّ نسوةٌ

لأنَّكِ مِنْ ضَوءٍ وغيرِكِ مِنْ عَتمِ

هَيولاكِ ظلٌّ راسمٌ لَكِ صُورةً

تَفوقُ مَدى فَهْمي وتَقْوى على عِلمي

وكيفَ إلى لُقياَي تأتينَ خِيفةً؟

وأنتِ وراءَ الشَكْلِ واللونِ والحَجْمِ!

When we meet,
we dwell together,
parallel,
not like lovers in an embrace.

We depart from our bodies
and we end our meeting,
to escape from our skeletons
of flesh and bones.

And when the continuous rain
ceases to pour,
and if my soul thirsts for it
but it does not fall,

I travel to your realm
in the form of a virgin cloud
so that I can be with you
without a body.

And in a hermitage,
in the world of souls,
we take refuge
to understand that which is beyond understanding.

وبعدَ تلاقينا، نُقيمُ معاً، ثُناً،

ولا نلتقي لُقيا الحبيبيْنِ.. بالضمِّ

ونَهْجُرُ جِسمَينا ونُنهي لِقاءَنا

ونَنْجو معاً مِنْ هيكلِ اللحْمِ والعَظمِ

وإنْ وَقَفَ الغيثُ الذي طالما همى

وإنْ عَطِشَتْ روحي إليهِ، ولَمْ يَهْمِ

أطيرُ إلى مَغْناكِ في جِسمِ غيمةٍ

بَتُولٍ، لِكيْ آتي إليكِ بِلا جِسمِ

وفي خَلوةٍ، في عالمِ الروحِ نَخْتَلي

وأرقى إلى فَهْمِ الدَقيقِ على الفَهْمِ

ABOUT THE POET
Youssef Abdul Samad

Born in Ras al Maten, Lebanon, Youssef
Abdul Samad immigrated to the USA in
1969. Today, he spends his time travelling
between the two countries. He says, "I am
made of a blend of the two worlds; when I
am in one place, I always find myself longing
for the other." Abdul Samad is a businessman
in New York City and has published five
volumes of Arabic poetry.

ABOUT THE TRANSLATOR
Ghada Alatrash

Daughter of former Syrian Ambassador Jabr
Al-Atrash, Ghada Alatrash immigrated with
her family from Syria to the United States in
1986. She holds a Master of Arts in English
from University of Oklahoma, USA. She
is an op/ed columnist for *Gulf News*, UAE,
and was previously op/ed columnist for
the *Cranbrook Daily Townsman*. She taught
English at Abu Dhabi Women's College,
UAE, and was an Adjunct Lecturer of Arabic
at University of Oklahoma. She has served
as a board member for the Multicultural
Advisory Board of British Columbia,
Canada. She is a member of the New Pen
League, New York. She currently resides in
BC, Canada. Email: *ghadaalatrash@live.com*
www.meaningwithinwords.blogspot.com

CPSIA information can be obtained at www.ICGtesting.com
Printed in the USA
LVOW070344090313

323430LV00005B/22/P